# THE ANGELIC ORDERS

## COSMIC SERVANTS OF THE INFINITE

MICHAEL VINCENT

# CONTENTS

# INTRODUCTION

## BEYOND WINGS AND HALOS

Everything you know about angels is wrong.

Not completely wrong—there are glimmers of truth in the traditional images. But the reality is so much bigger and more magnificent than cherubs on clouds or warriors with flaming swords. Angels are more profound than what religion has made them and more beautiful than art has depicted them. They are more than vague spiritual presences or poetic metaphors for goodness.

Angels are real. They have names, orders, personalities, and purposes. They exist in countless varieties, each designed for particular functions in a vast cosmic administration. They work in teams, follow hierarchies, and carry out missions with precision. They are as literal as you are, just operating in dimensions you cannot yet perceive.

This book will tell you what I believe to be the truth about angels. It will present a broad but detailed, inspiring yet specific account of angels and provide a coherent framework for understanding angelic reality. It does not prove the unprovable. But it's possibly the most comprehensive description of angels available. Consider this description of their nature:

*Angels do not have material bodies, but they are definite and discrete beings; they are of spirit nature and origin. They are very affectionate and sympathetic beings, but they are not sex-emotion creatures.*

*Though invisible to mortals, they perceive you as you are in the flesh; they intellectually understand the mode of mortal life, and they share all of man's nonsensuous emotions and sentiments.*

*They appreciate and greatly enjoy your efforts in music, art, and real humor. They are fully cognizant of your moral struggles and spiritual difficulties. They love human beings, and only good can result from your efforts to understand and love them.*[1]

This book is not my personal insight or theological speculation. I am presenting information from a source that provides unprecedented detail about cosmic reality. My role is interpreter and curator, not originator.

1

---

# THE ORIGIN OF ANGELS

Angels are eternal, and they were created—brought into existence at a specific moment for a specific purpose.

Unlike God, who has always existed, they have beginnings. Unlike humans, who evolve through biological processes, angels are created fully formed, with complete personalities and immediate awareness of their identity. They do not grow up. They do not learn to become themselves. They simply *are*, from the moment of creation.

But who creates them? And why are there so many different kinds?

## THE SOURCE

At the center of all angelic creation stands the Infinite Spirit—the Third Person of the Trinity, equal with the Universal Father and the Eternal Son. The Infinite Spirit is God in motion—the divine hand that translates infinite thought into finite action. While the Father conceives and the Son embodies, the Spirit orchestrates. He conducts the cosmic symphony. Every angel in existence carries a spark of his kinetic purpose.

And he is the source of angels.

The Infinite Spirit creates them to be his ministers throughout creation. Each angelic order expresses different aspects of his nature. They are, in a sense, the Infinite Spirit's hands extended into every corner of the universe.

The highest angels—the supernaphim of Paradise—are created directly by the Infinite Spirit himself. These are the most magnificent, the most capable, and the most divinely perfect of the spirit helpers. They serve on Paradise and on the billion perfect worlds of the central universe. They minister to perfected beings and to ascending mortals who have nearly completed their journey.

But the Infinite Spirit does not create all angels personally. He delegates this creative prerogative to other high beings who act as extensions of his creative power.

## THE UNIVERSE MOTHER SPIRIT

In each local universe—and there are hundreds of thousands of local universes—the Creative Spirit creates the angels native to that universe. This Creative Spirit is the local universe representative of the Infinite Spirit, a unique divine being who partners with the Creator Son to bring forth and sustain their universe.

She is called the Universe Mother Spirit, and she is the direct creator of the seraphim and other angelic orders native to her universe. These angels possess remarkable abilities:

> *The seraphim are so created as to function on both spiritual and literal levels. There are few phases of morontia (semi-spirit) or spirit activity which are not open to their ministrations. While in personal status angels are not so far removed from human beings, in certain functional performances seraphim far transcend them. They possess many powers far beyond human comprehension.*

> *For example: You have been told that the "very hairs of your head are numbered," and it is true they are, but a seraphim does not spend her time counting them and keeping the number corrected up to date.*

*Angels possess inherent and automatic (that is, automatic as far as you could perceive) powers of knowing such things; you would truly regard a seraphim as a mathematical prodigy. Therefore, numerous duties which would be tremendous tasks for mortals are performed with exceeding ease by seraphim.*[1]

When the Divine Minister creates a seraphim, a new consciousness ignites—complete from the first instant, eager to learn her role in the vast machinery of divine administration.

These beings are created in enormous numbers. In our universe alone, there are more than 71 billion. They toil in countless capacities —as guardians, teachers, administrators, recorders, and ministers. They are the primary workforce that makes mortal ascension achievable.

*Seraphim are projected in unit formation—41,472 at a time—ever since the creation of the pattern angels and certain angelic archetypes in the early times of this universe.*[2]

This Divine Mother doesn't create seraphim randomly. She creates them as needed to fulfill specific functions in the ongoing administration and ministry of the local universe.

This is not automatic or mechanical. The Mother Spirit is a person, and her creative acts are personal. She knows each creature she creates. She cares about them individually. She guides their development and follows their careers with maternal interest.

## OTHER CREATIVE SOURCES

Different orders of angels have different origins:

**Supernaphim** are created by the Infinite Spirit (primary supernaphim) or by the Seven Master Spirits and the Reflective Spirits (secondary and tertiary supernaphim). They are the angels of Paradise and the central universe.

**Seconaphim** are created by the Reflective Spirits and serve in the seven superuniverses, the vast divisions of creation that surround the central universe.

**Tertiaphim** are created by the Infinite Spirit and certain high superuniverse personalities. They are liaisons between the local universes and the superuniverse administration.

**Omniaphim** are created exclusively by the Infinite Spirit and live as his personal aids in certain high functions.

**Seraphim**, as mentioned, are created by the Universe Mother Spirit of each local universe.

**Cherubim and sanobim** are also created by the Universe Mother Spirit, specifically as helpers and associates for seraphim.

Each order has its own origin, but all trace back ultimately to the Infinite Spirit—the God of action, who coordinates all that is done throughout creation.

## ANGELIC TRAINING

These celestial persons undergo immense training prior to functioning in their assigned roles. A guardian seraphim must be capable and wise before she's assigned to a human. An administrative angel must understand cosmic protocol before engaging in universe administration. Their training follows a specific pattern:

*Seraphim spend their first millennium as noncommissioned observers on the universe capital and its associated world schools. The second millennium is spent on the seraphic worlds of the headquarters circuit.*

*At the termination of this period of training, seraphim are mobilized in the conventional groups and units of the angelic organization and are assigned to some one of the constellations.*

*Seraphim are initiated as ministering spirits by serving as observers on the lowest of the evolutionary worlds. After this experience they return to the associate worlds of the headquarters of the assigned constellation to begin their advanced studies and more definitely to prepare for service in some particular local system.*

While angels do not evolve as humans do, many orders—especially seraphim—have enormous potential for development. They can advance through multiple levels of achievement and eventually ascend to Paradise as do mortals. Cherubim can evolve into seraphim. Some undergo dramatic transformations in capability and status.

## Personality and Choice

When the Universe Mother Spirit creates a seraphim, she brings forth a new person. That person has her own temperament, her own interests, her own way of approaching problems, her own style of ministry. She has preferences. She has emotional responses. She has the capacity to form relationships, to bond with other beings, to develop deep attachments.

Angels are not robots. They are persons.

Your guardian seraphim, for instance, has a name. She has a history—experiences, relationships, achievements. She has chosen to act as a guardian rather than in some other capacity. She has accepted assignment to you specifically, and that assignment means something to her. You are not just a case file or a duty. You are her sacred trust, her mission, the soul she has covenanted to help survive.

This volitional personality comes directly from the creative act. It is not an accident or an afterthought. It's essential to their nature and their function.

Because angels are persons—real beings with minds and wills—they possess genuine agency. They can choose. They are not compelled to serve, not programmed to obey. Their loyalty is volitional, their service is freely given.

This freedom makes their ministry meaningful. Obedience from a creature without free will has no moral value. But an angel who chooses to serve, who remains faithful through difficulty, who gives herself to ministry out of genuine love—that choice carries weight.

And because choice is real, the possibility of wrong choice exists. Most angels, across vast distances and countless ages, remain faithful. But not all. In the history of this universe, there have been angels who chose self will over divine will, who rejected their purpose and pursued other aims. These unfortunate events are rare, but they happen.

The fact that rebellion is possible makes angelic loyalty profound rather than inevitable. Your guardian angel is with you not because she must be, but because she chooses to be. That makes all the difference.

## The Reason for Angels

Why does the Infinite Spirit create angels at all? Why not handle everything himself?

Because the universe is vast beyond human comprehension. There are trillions of inhabited worlds. There are countless mortals ascending from animal origin toward divine destiny. There are endless tasks to complete, endless needs to meet, endless opportunities for service.

One being, even a divine being, cannot personally minister to every individual across all creation. Distribution is necessary. Delegation is required.

So the Infinite Spirit creates angels—beings who carry his nature, who express his will, who extend his ministry into every corner of existence. Through them, the personal touch of divinity reaches every ascending soul. Through them, no mortal is left unattended, no sincere seeker is ignored, no worthy effort goes unnoticed.

Angels are God's answer to the problem of scale. How do you provide personal care to trillions of individuals across vast distances and stages of growth? You create personal ministers—countless millions of them, each capable of forming genuine relationships, each dedicated to serving specific souls or functions.

This is not cold efficiency. This is infinite love expressed through infinite creativity. The Infinite Spirit creates them because he cares about everyone, and he wants every person to receive personal attention, personal guidance, personal help.

Your guardian angel exists because God loves you enough to ensure you have someone who knows you completely and works tirelessly on your behalf. When you die, angels will be the first beings you encounter. Your guardian will be there, along with others who facilitate your transition to the next life.

---

That's the origin of angels. Not myth, not poetry, but actual divine creativity expressed in millions upon millions of unique, intelligent, loving beings who exist to serve.

You may wonder why, if angels are so active, you cannot see them. We'll address this reality later—but know that invisibility does not mean inaction. They're here, working all around you, whether you perceive them or not.

The word 'angels' is too simple and broad. There are orders within orders, each with distinct capabilities and assignments. Let's begin at the top of this vast hierarchy—with the angels of Paradise.

To understand the angels closest to you, you must first grasp the full scope of angelic reality. We begin at the top and descend toward Earth. If you prefer to start with the angels closer to home, skip ahead to Chapter 10 and work backward. The architecture will make more sense when you return.

Everything we're about to explore—the vast hierarchies, the cosmic geography, the grandeur you cannot yet imagine—exists ultimately for one purpose: your eternal journey.

2

# SUPERNAPHIM

## ANGELS OF PARADISE

At the very top of the angelic hierarchy stand the supernaphim—the most exalted, most capable, most magnificent angels in all existence. Paradise itself and the billion perfect worlds of the central universe provide the primary arena of their living and working. As ministers of perfection, these beings serve perfected personalities and guide ascending mortals who have nearly completed their journey from animal origin to divine destiny. Their ministry extends throughout creation:

> *Supernaphim are the ministering spirits of Paradise and the central universe; they are the highest order of the lowest group of the children of the Infinite Spirit—the angelic hosts. Such ministering spirits are to be encountered from the Isle of Paradise to the worlds of time and space. No major part of the organized and inhabited creation is without their services.*[1]

You will meet them eventually, and when you do, you'll understand what angelic ministry looks like at its absolute finest.

Supernaphim exist in three distinct categories, each with different origins and functions:

**Primary supernaphim** are created directly by the Infinite Spirit himself. The oldest, most experienced ministers in existence—as close to divine perfection as created beings can be—these superangels serve on Paradise, the eternal Isle at the center of all things, ministering to the Trinity, the Paradise citizens, and the ascending pilgrims who finally reach the goal of their long journey.

**Secondary supernaphim** are created by the Seven Master Spirits, the highest personalities of the Infinite Spirit. These superangels serve in Havona, the billion perfect worlds that encircle Paradise. They minister to the natives of Havona and to ascending mortals as they traverse the seven circuits of the central universe.

**Tertiary supernaphim** are created by the Reflective Spirits and by certain secondary supernaphim who have achieved special status. They also serve in Havona, functioning as assistants and helpers in the ministry to ascending pilgrims.

All three orders are supernaphim—all are exalted beyond description. But they have different roles, different assignments, different relationships with those they encounter.

## Primary Supernaphim: Paradise Ministers

The primary supernaphim have existed since the early days of eternity. They are specialists performing the highest forms of spiritual ministry.

These superaphic beings divide into seven orders, each mastering a different dimension of Paradise ministry—worship, wisdom, knowledge, conduct, ethics, assignment, and rest. Seven keys, seven gates, seven paths by which perfected beings experience the source of creation at the very center of reality.

**Conductors of Worship** help beings experience the ultimate joy of divine communion.

> *Worship is the conscious and joyous act of recognizing and acknowledging the truth and fact of the intimate and personal relationships of the Creators with their creatures.*
>
> *The quality of worship is determined by the depth of creature perception; and as the knowledge of the infinite character of the Gods progresses, the act of worship becomes increasingly all-encompassing until it eventually attains the glory of the highest experiential delight and the most exquisite pleasure known to created beings.[2]*

**Masters of Philosophy** coordinate wisdom. Helping beings understand profound truths, integrate vast knowledge, and develop cosmic perspective stands as their primary function. As teachers of the highest order, this corps instructs through dimensions of reality that transcend words.

> *Never do you climb so high or advance so far that there do not remain a thousand mysteries which demand the employment of philosophy in an attempted solution.*
>
> *The master philosophers of Paradise delight to lead the minds of its inhabitants, both native and ascendant, in the exhilarating pursuit of attempting to solve universe problems.*
>
> *These superaphic masters of philosophy are the "wise men of heaven," the beings of wisdom who make use of the truth of knowledge and the facts of experience in their efforts to master the unknown. With them knowledge attains to truth and experience ascends to wisdom.[3]*

**Custodians of Knowledge** preserve and organize information. Paradise is the repository of all significant knowledge in the universes of time and space, and these angels manage that repository, making information accessible to those who need it.

*The superaphic custodians of knowledge are the higher "living epistles" known and read by all who dwell on Paradise. They are the divine records of truth, the living books of real knowledge.*

*You have heard about records in the "book of life." The custodians of knowledge are just such living books, records of perfection imprinted upon the eternal tablets of divine life and supreme surety. They are in reality living, automatic libraries.*

*The facts of the universes are inherent in these primary supernaphim, actually recorded in these angels; and it is also inherently impossible for an untruth to gain lodgment in the minds of these perfect and replete repositories of the truth of eternity and the intelligence of time.*[4]

**Directors of Conduct** help perfected beings navigate the social protocols of Paradise. Even in perfection, there are appropriate ways to to behave, to interact, to be.

*The ascendant mortals find it helpful to receive the counsel of the superaphic directors of conduct, who instruct the new members of Paradise society in the usages of the perfect conduct of the high beings who sojourn on the central Isle of Light and Life.*

*Harmony is the keynote of the central universe, and detectable order prevails on Paradise.*

*Proper conduct is essential to progress by way of knowledge, through philosophy, to the spiritual heights of spontaneous worship. There is a divine technique in the approach to Divinity; and the acquirement of this technique must await the pilgrims' arrival on Paradise.*[5]

**Interpreters of Ethics** help beings understand the rightness of actions in the context of eternal values. They don't impose rules; they help others see why certain choices align with divine goodness and others don't.

*The interpreters of ethics are of inestimable assistance to the Paradise arrivals in helping them to adjust to numerous groups of majestic beings during that eventful period extending from the attainment of residential status to formal induction into the Corps of Mortal Finaliters.*[6]

**Chiefs of Assignment** coordinate service. Every being on Paradise serves—it's the nature of perfected existence.

*Study and instruction are not the exclusive occupations of Paradise arrivals; service also plays its essential part in the educational experiences of Paradise.*[7]

**Instigators of Rest**. Even perfected beings need rest—not from physical fatigue, but from the intensity of eternal worship and service. These angels facilitate rejuvenation, ensuring that work remains joyful rather than burdensome.

*The one essential to the enjoyment of Paradise is rest, divine rest; and these instigators of rest are the final instructors who make ready the pilgrims of time for their introduction to eternity.*

*They begin their work on the final attainment circle of the central universe and continue it when the pilgrim awakes from the last transition sleep, the slumber which graduates a creature of space into the realm of the eternal.*[8]

The primary supernaphim's existence revolves around maintaining the highest possible quality of experience for those who dwell at the center of creation. Mastery of their craft spans ages too long for mortal comprehension, the art of ministry perfected through eons of service.

## Secondary Supernaphim: Havona Guides

The secondary supernaphim assist ascending mortals as they traverse Havona—the billion perfect worlds arranged in seven concentric circuits around Paradise. Every pilgrim must pass through these circuits, learning profound lessons at each level, before reaching Paradise itself.

And at every circuit, secondary supernaphim provide guidance. They organize into seven groups corresponding to the seven circuits of Havona:

**Pilgrim Helpers** greet ascending mortals when they first arrive in Havona from the time space creations. These angels help new arrivals adjust to the perfect central universe. They explain what's expected, what opportunities exist, what the journey ahead will require. They are welcoming, patient, and expertly skilled at helping ascendant beings feel at home in perfection.

**Supremacy Guides** work on the sixth Havona circuit, where mortal pilgrims begin to understand the Supreme Being—God evolving through the experiences of all creation. This is complex theology made real, and these angels help mortals grasp what intellectual effort alone could never achieve.

**Trinity Guides** labor on the fifth circuit, preparing the ascenders for the recognition of the Paradise Trinity. Understanding three infinite persons functioning as one God is not simple, even for those who have ascended from animal origin through countless worlds on high. They make the incomprehensible accessible.

**Son Finders** minister on the fourth circuit, helping to achieve a new understanding of the Eternal Son—the second person of the Trinity. This isn't mere intellectual knowledge; it's experiential recognition. These angels facilitate that experience.

**Father Guides** will be found on the third circuit, preparing ascending mortals for the ultimate encounter—meeting God the Father face to face. This preparation requires profound support. These angels know how to ready a soul for the greatest moment of its existence.

**Counselors and Advisers** work on the second circuit, helping to integrate everything that's been learned. They answer final questions and resolve lingering confusions, ensuring that each soul is truly ready for Paradise.

**Complements of Rest** serve on the first and innermost circuit of Havona. Here, ascendant mortals receive their final preparation for Paradise admission. These angels provide profound rest—not sleep, but deep spiritual rejuvenation that readies the soul for translation to Paradise itself.

When you reach Havona, millions of years from now, you will meet these angels. They will guide you through challenges you cannot yet imagine. They will help you understand truths that currently lie beyond your grasp. They will celebrate with you when you finally stand on Paradise, having completed the longest journey in all creation.

## TERTIARY SUPERNAPHIM: THE ASSISTANTS

The tertiary supernaphim perform as assistants throughout Havona. They help the secondary supernaphim in their ministry to ascending pilgrims. They handle countless administrative and coordinating functions that make the smooth operation of the central universe feasible. They are the supporting cast that ensures every ascending mortal receives exactly the help needed at exactly the right moment.

Some tertiary supernaphim serve as messengers, carrying communications between the Havona worlds. Some work as recorders, preserving the experiences of ascending pilgrims. Some labor as coordinators, arranging meetings, scheduling training, ensuring that nothing falls through the cracks. Their ministry is comprehensive:

*These servants of the Seven Master Spirits are the angelic specialists of the various circuits of Havona, and their ministry extends to both the ascending pilgrims of time and the descending pilgrims of eternity.*

*On the billion study worlds of the perfect central creation, your superaphic associates of all orders will be fully visible to you. There you will all be, in the highest sense, fraternal and understanding beings of mutual contact and sympathy.*

*You will also fully recognize and exquisitely fraternize with the descending pilgrims, the Paradise Citizens, who traverse these circuits from within outward, entering Havona through the pilot world of the first circuit and proceeding outward to the seventh.*[9]

This is one of the joys awaiting you in Havona — not just receiving ministry, but truly knowing your ministers. The tertiary supernaphim will not be distant administrators. They will be companions you recognize, understand, and appreciate. The barriers that separate mortals from angels in the material realms will have dissolved entirely.

## YOUR SUPERNAPHIM ENCOUNTER

Your exalted encounters with the high supernaphim may not happen for a very long time. You will first survive death, move through the mansion worlds, advance through your local universe, traverse your superuniverse, and finally enter Havona. This will take millions of years by Earth time, though you'll experience it very differently.

But when you finally engage with the supernaphim, you'll understand what angelic ministry looks like when perfected. You'll see what it means to be served by beings who have been doing this work since the dawn of time. You'll experience guidance so expert, so personal, so perfectly attuned to your needs that you'll wonder how you ever managed without it.

The supernaphim disclose that God sees immense value in you. He doesn't just provide minimal help to get you through. He provides the absolute best assistance available at every stage of your ascension. When you reach the central universe, you will be guided by angels who are the finest in all creation—not because you've earned it, but because that's the quality of care God extends to all his ascending children.

The supernaphim are waiting for you. They've been waiting since before you were born. They will wait as long as necessary. And when you finally arrive, they will greet you with joy and guide you through the final stages of your incomprehensible journey from animal origin to Paradise citizenship.

That's what the angels of Paradise do. And they do it with a skill and devotion that can only be called perfect.

3

___________

# SECONAPHIM

## THE REFLECTIVE ANGELS

Beyond Paradise and the central universe lie the seven superuniverses—each containing hundreds of billions of inhabited worlds. These are the realms of time and space where evolution occurs, where imperfect mortals begin their journey toward perfection.

And serving throughout these superuniverses are the seconaphim—angels of extraordinary capability who facilitate communication, conduct administration, and provide specialized ministry to both ascending mortals and superuniverse administrators.

The seconaphim possess an ability that sets them apart from all other angels: they can reflect. They are living mirrors of truth, able to capture and display information, wisdom, and even the very thoughts of distant beings. They are the communication network of the superuniverses, the means by which the vast distances and countless worlds remain connected and coordinated.

## ORIGINS

Seconaphim are created by the Reflective Spirits—unique beings who dwell on the headquarters worlds of the seven superuniverses. These Reflective Spirits possess the remarkable ability to simultaneously reflect everything that occurs throughout their entire superuniverse. They can access all that happens in their domain, and can make that knowledge available to those who need it.

But the Reflective Spirits are far more than cosmic transmitters or information relays. They are living personalities who possess consciousness and memory:

> *They are not merely transmitting agents; they are retentive personali-*
> *ties as well. Their offspring, the seconaphim, are also retentive or*
> *record personalities.*[1]

This means both parent and offspring don't just pass information along—they preserve it, remember it, understand it. They are living repositories of knowledge, not passive channels. The seconaphim inherit this capacity from their creators: the ability to retain what they reflect.

## LIVING RECORDS

The seconaphim serve a unique function in the cosmic record-keeping system:

> *Everything of true spiritual value is registered in duplicate, and one*
> *impression is preserved in the personal equipment of some member of*
> *one of the numerous orders of secoraphic personalities belonging to*
> *the vast staff of the Reflective Spirits.*[2]

Think about what this means. Every genuinely important spiritual event, decision, or achievement is recorded twice—once in formal records, and once in the living mind of a seconaphim. Nothing of real value is ever lost.

> *The formal records of the universes are passed up by and through the angelic recorders, but the true spiritual records are assembled by reflectivity and are preserved in the minds of suitable and appropriate personalities belonging to the family of the Infinite Spirit.*

> *These are the live records in contrast with the formal and dead records of the universe, and they are perfectly preserved in the living minds of the recording personalities of the Infinite Spirit.*[3]

The formal archives contain data—names, dates, and events recorded mechanically. But the seconaphim preserve something more: the meaning, the spiritual significance, the living truth behind the facts. They don't just store information. They understand it, hold it in conscious awareness, keep it alive in their minds.

Your spiritual journey is not just filed away in some cosmic database. It's held in the living consciousness of a seconaphim who comprehends what your choices mean, who recognizes your growth, who preserves the truth of who you're becoming.

## The Cosmic Information Network

There is another vital function this enterprise provides:

> *The reflectivity organization is also the news-gathering and the decree-disseminating mechanism of all creation. It is in constant operation in contrast with the periodic functioning of the various broadcast services.*[4]

This is the universe's communication infrastructure, operating continuously. When celestial authorities need to know what's happening across immeasurable distances, they consult the reflectivity system. When important decisions or decrees must be transmitted, this organization carries them instantly across creation.

And here's what makes this system remarkable: it's volitional.

> *The reflectivity service is apparently automatic or self-operating, but it is not. It is all very personal and intelligent; its precision results from perfection of personality cooperation.*[5]

The system works with such flawless coordination that it seems mechanical. But it's actually the result of countless personalities working together in perfect harmony. Every transmission is personal. Every reflection involves conscious intelligence. The precision comes not from machinery but from perfected cooperation between living minds.

> *The Reflective Spirits themselves are true personalities but of such an order as to be incomprehensible to material beings.*[6]

We can barely comprehend what the Reflective Spirits are. But we might understand their offspring, the seconaphim, who inherit and transmit this reflective ability.

> *The attribute of reflectivity, the phenomenon of the mind levels of the Infinite Spirit, the Supreme Being, and the Master Spirits, is transmissible to all beings concerned in the working of this vast scheme of universal intelligence.*[7]

Reflectivity itself is a divine attribute, originating at the highest levels of cosmic reality. And it flows downward, becoming available to those beings whose function requires it.

The seconaphim possess a focalized version of this remarkable ability. Each seconaphim can function as a specialized mirror, reflecting specific types of information or insight. Each becomes a living lens—capturing wisdom from across the cosmos and projecting it into the minds of those who need it. They become living channels through which truth, knowledge, and wisdom flow across the universe domains.

There are three orders of seconaphim, each with different functions
and capabilities.

## PRIMARY SECONAPHIM: LIVING MIRRORS

These exalted angels serve the highest time space administration
directly at the headquarters of each superuniverse.

> *The primary seconaphim, of assignment to the Ancients of Days,
> are living mirrors in the service of these triune rulers. Think what
> it means in the economy of a superuniverse to be able to turn, as it
> were, to a living mirror and therein to see and therewith to hear the
> certain responses of another being a thousand or a hundred thou-
> sand light-years distant and to do all this instantly and
> unerringly.*[8]

The rulers of these superuniverses are the Ancients of Days — the
oldest and most powerful beings in the time-space realms. Each superuniverse is governed by three Ancients of Days, who hold supreme
judicial authority over their domain. They alone render final judgment on matters of eternal survival. Their decisions are absolute,
their wisdom beyond question. And serving these triune rulers are the
primary seconaphim.

Seven specialized types of primary seconaphim serve the Ancients of
Days:

**The Voice of the Conjoint Actor** reflects the mind and will of the
Infinite Spirit, ensuring that superuniverse rulers remain aligned with
the purposes of the Third Source and Center.

**The Voice of the Seven Master Spirits** reflects the combined wisdom
and directives of those supreme beings who channel the sevenfold
nature of Deity to the superuniverses.

**The Voice of the Creator Sons** reflects the thoughts and intentions of
the divine Sons who rule the local universes, keeping superuniverse
administration informed of developments throughout their domains.

**The Voice of the Angelic Hosts** reflects the collective activities and status of the countless angels serving throughout the superuniverse — a living summary of angelic ministry across billions of worlds.

**Broadcast Receivers** function as living reception centers for important communications arriving through the reflectivity circuits from Paradise and Havona.

**Transport Personalities** serve specialized transit functions, facilitating the movement of certain beings who cannot be transported by other means.

**The Reserve Corps** stands ready for emergency assignments, available when unexpected needs arise in superuniverse administration.

Through these seven orders, the Ancients of Days maintain perfect awareness of everything relevant to their governance. No significant development escapes their attention. No critical decision lacks adequate information. The primary seconaphim make omniscient administration possible within the limits of time and space.


## Secondary Seconaphim: Reflectors of Truth

These angels organize into seven types, each reflecting a different category of information:

**The Voice of Wisdom** reflects the accumulated wisdom of creation. When administrators need insight into how to handle complex situations, these beings provide access to the collective experience and judgment of all who have faced similar challenges before.

> *The Voices of Wisdom are living, current, replete, and thoroughly reliable concentrations and focalizations of the co-ordinated wisdom of the universe of universes. To the well-nigh infinite volume of information circulating on the master circuits of the superuniverses, these superb beings are so reflective and selective, so sensitive, as to be able*

*to segregate and receive the essence of wisdom and unerringly to transmit these jewels of mentation.*[9]

**The Soul of Philosophy** reflects coordinated understanding. They help integrate diverse knowledge into coherent perspective, ensuring that decisions align with ultimate values and cosmic purpose.

*Think of stepping up to a huge living mirror, as it were, but instead of beholding the likeness of your finite and material self, of perceiving a reflection of the wisdom of divinity and the philosophy of Paradise.*[10]

**The Union of Souls** reflects group consciousness. They can show what multiple beings collectively think or feel about a matter, revealing consensus or highlighting points of disagreement that need resolution.

*Of all the problems in the universe requiring an exercise of the consummate wisdom of experience and adaptability, none are more important than those arising out of the relationships and associations of intelligent beings.*

*The spheres of perfection are manned by those who have mastered this art of working with other beings. Few are the duties in the universe for the lone servant. The higher you ascend, the more lonely you become when temporarily without the association of your fellows.*[11]

**The Heart of Counsel** reflects advisory wisdom. They provide access to the best guidance available on any matter, drawing from the accumulated counsel of countless advisers.

*Whenever the Divine Counselors are called upon for important advice or decisions, they immediately requisition an ensemble of the Hearts of Counsel, and presently there is handed down a ruling which actually incorporates the co-ordinated wisdom and advice of the most competent minds of the entire superuniverse.*[12]

**The Joy of Existence** reflects positive reality. They show what's working, what's good, what brings joy and satisfaction.

> *Their principal activities are directed toward promoting reactions of joy among the various orders of the angelic hosts and the lower will creatures. They function as joy clearinghouses, seeking to upstep the pleasure reactions of the realms while trying to improve the humor taste, to develop a superhumor among mortals and angels.*[13]

**The Satisfaction of Service** reflects the fulfillment that comes from meaningful work. They help beings understand the value of their contributions and experience the deep satisfaction of serving the greater good.

> *They strive to enhance the value of service and to augment the satisfactions to be derived therefrom. They have done much to illuminate the deferred rewards inherent in service for the extension of the kingdom of truth. And by using the performances of the best to inspire and encourage the mediocre, these seconaphim contribute immensely to the quality of devoted service.*
>
> *Effective use is made of the fraternal competitive spirit by circulating to any one world information about what the others, particularly the best, are doing. A refreshing and wholesome rivalry is promoted even among the seraphic hosts.*[14]

**The Discerner of Spirits** reflects spiritual authenticity. They can reveal the true motivations and spiritual status of beings, helping administrators understand who is genuine and who might be deceptive.

> *Regardless of the source or channel of information, no matter how meager the evidence at hand, when it is subjected to their reflective scrutiny, these discerners will forthwith inform us as to the true motive, the actual purpose, and the real nature of its origin.*[15]

The seconaphim are of tremendous assistance to superuniverse administration. Without them, these supercreations could not be effectively governed. With them, no significant matter escapes attention, no critical information remains unavailable, no important decision lacks adequate counsel.

## Tertiary Seconaphim: Specialized Servants

The tertiary seconaphim act in various specialized capacities throughout the superuniverse. Some work as messengers, carrying information between worlds. Some toil as recorders, preserving important events and decisions. Some harmonize between different administrative levels, ensuring smooth communication and cooperation.

They are the supporting infrastructure that keeps the superuniverse functioning efficiently. They're less visible than their primary and secondary counterparts, but absolutely essential to the operation of superuniverse administration and the care of ascending mortals.

**The Significance of Origins.** These reflective beings maintain living genealogies of a vast host of beings, instantly providing complete ancestry and current status information to universe administrators who need it.

> *All relationships and the application of ethics grow out of the fundamental facts of origin. Origin is the basis of the relational reaction of the Gods. These seconaphim are always ready to supply an up-to-date, replete, and trustworthy estimate of the ancestral factors and the current actual status of any individual on any world; and their computation of possessed facts is always up to the minute.*[16]

**The Memory of Mercy.** These seconaphim keep living records of all mercy extended to individuals and races, maintaining a spiritual trial balance that discloses whether divine compassion has been fairly distributed and faithfully received.

> *The Memory of Mercy discloses the moral debt of the children of mercy—their spiritual liabilities—to be set down against their assets of the saving provision established by the Sons of God.*

> *In accordance with the findings of the Significance of Origins, a mercy credit is established for the survival of each rational creature, a credit of lavish proportions and one of sufficient grace to insure the survival of every soul who really desires divine citizenship.*[17]

**The Import of Time.** These angels evaluate how time has been used by ascending mortals, testifying in cosmic courts about whether individuals had adequate opportunity for spiritual decisions and forecasting how much time future undertakings will require.

> *You will first encounter these beings on the mansion worlds, and they will there instruct you in the advantageous use of that which you call "time," both in its positive employment, work, and in its negative utilization, rest. Both uses of time are important.*[18]

**The Solemnity of Trust.** These seconaphim measure trustworthiness with perfect accuracy, weighing character in living scales so that administrators can assign responsibilities appropriately without overloading individuals or risking betrayal.

> *It is the plan of your superiors to advance you by augmented trusts just as fast as your character is sufficiently developed to gracefully bear these added responsibilities, but to overload the individual only courts disaster and insures disappointment.*[19]

**The Sanctity of Service.** These celestial servants reveal the true nature and hidden motives behind any act of service, showing whether ministry springs from genuine love or from selfish ambition, making them the mind readers and heart searchers of the universe.

*Service—purposeful service, not slavery—is productive of the highest satisfaction and is expressive of the divinest dignity. Service—more service, increased service, difficult service, adventurous service, and at last divine and perfect service—is the goal of time and the destination of space.*

*The universal economy is based on intake and output; throughout the eternal career you will never encounter monotony of inaction or stagnation of personality. Progress is made possible by inherent motion, advancement grows out of the divine capacity for action, and achievement is the child of imaginative adventure.*[20]

**The Secret of Greatness.** These seconaphim measure true greatness by assessing unselfishness and self-control, reflecting the quality of character that makes beings worthy of increased responsibility.

**The Soul of Goodness.** These angels work inseparably with the Secret of Greatness to evaluate divine goodness in individuals, demonstrating that true greatness and genuine goodness cannot be divorced from one another and are always found together in God-like beings.

*Greatness is synonymous with divinity. The more steadfastly you behold, and the more persistently you pursue, the concepts of divine goodness, the more certainly will you grow in greatness, in true magnitude of genuine survival character.*[21]

## THE TECHNOLOGY OF REFLECTIVITY

How do seconaphim reflect? What does this actually mean?

Seconaphim literally function as receivers and transmitters of information. They can access knowledge from across the superuniverse. They can display, in real time, what's happening on distant worlds. They can make visible the thoughts and intentions of beings light-years away. They can reveal the accumulated wisdom of millions of years of experience.

This is not technology in the mechanical sense—it's a spiritual capacity, an inherent ability built into their nature. But it functions with the precision and reliability of the best technology. When a seconaphim reflects, what appears is accurate, immediate, and complete.

This reflective capacity makes the seconaphim indispensable. In a superuniverse spanning vast distances and containing billions of inhabited worlds, communication would otherwise be impossibly slow. Messages would take years to travel. Administrators would make decisions based on hopelessly outdated information. Coordination would collapse.

The seconaphim solve this problem. Through them, the superuniverse remains connected. Knowledge flows freely. Wisdom accumulates and becomes accessible. Administration functions with efficiency that would otherwise be impossible.

## The Importance of Reflectivity

When you reach your superuniverse headquarters, millions of years into your ascension, you will see seconaphim in action. You'll watch them reflect information from worlds you've never heard of. You'll experience their love personally as they help you develop wisdom and discernment. You'll understand that the universe is not fragmented or isolated but deeply connected, with information and truth flowing constantly through angelic channels.

This should give you tremendous confidence. The universe is properly managed. It's not running on guesswork or outdated information. Divine administration operates with perfect knowledge, perfect insight, perfect coordination—made realizable by angels who can reflect reality itself.

The seconaphim display the import placed upon divine governance. God establishes systems of administration so sophisticated, so effective, that nothing of importance escapes notice and no legitimate need goes unmet.

You are part of a cosmos where truth is accessible, where wisdom accumulates, where knowledge flows freely to those who need it. And one day, you'll benefit directly from their extraordinary abilities.

From the superuniverse level where seconaphim work, let's descend one step closer to home.

4

---

# BRILLIANT EVENING STARS

The Brilliant Evening Stars are among the most exalted beings created by the Creator Son and the Universe Mother Spirit. They are not angels in the technical sense—they are higher than angels, operating at administrative and advisory levels that angels rarely reach. But they work closely with angels, and their work affects the lives of ascending mortals in profound ways. This is an elite order:

> *The Brilliant Evening Stars are a unique twofold order, embracing some of created dignity and others of attained service. The local universe corps of these superangels now numbers 13,641. There are 4,832 of created dignity, while 8,809 are ascendant spirits who have attained this goal of exalted service.*
>
> *Many of these ascendant Evening Stars started their universe careers as seraphim; others have ascended from unrevealed levels of creature life. As an attainment goal this high corps is never closed to ascension candidates so long as a universe is not settled in light and life.*[1]

There are relatively few Brilliant Evening Stars in the entire local universe. Each one is unique, powerful, and entrusted with responsibilities that require wisdom, judgment, and absolute reliability. They possess a spirit force which can be manifested regardless of their personal presence.


## Created for Leadership

Brilliant Evening Stars serve in high capacities—as advisers to system sovereigns, as coordinators between different levels of administration, as special representatives handling complex situations that require exceptional wisdom and authority. They even accompany bestowal Sons on their planetary missions to improve the spiritual evolution of the races.

They are high administrators who, among other things, ensure that the systems serving mortals function properly. They work at levels where decisions affect millions of worlds and trillions of beings. Their ministry is remote from individual human concerns, but its effects ripple down to touch every ascending soul.


## Liaison and Coordination

One of the primary functions of Brilliant Evening Stars is to act as liaisons between different orders of beings and different levels of administration. They translate between Paradise authorities and local universe administrators. They coordinate between the Creator Son's government and the system sovereigns who manage individual star systems. They facilitate communication and cooperation across vast organizational distances.

This liaison work is essential. The universe is not a simple hierarchy where orders flow smoothly from top to bottom. It's a complex network of semi-autonomous authorities, each with specific jurisdictions and responsibilities. Keeping this network functioning harmoniously requires skilled coordinators who understand multiple perspectives and can facilitate effective communication between very different types of beings.

Brilliant Evening Stars excel at this work. They have the wisdom to see multiple viewpoints simultaneously, the diplomatic skill to help different jurisdictions cooperate, and the authority to make their coordination efforts effective.

## RELATION TO ANGELS

Brilliant Evening Stars supervise much of the angelic work. Seraphim report through organizational channels that ultimately reach Brilliant Evening Stars. Administrative decisions are often made by or with the advice of these high beings. The smooth functioning of the angelic system depends on the quality of administration that Brilliant Evening Stars provide.

Additionally, understanding that beings of this caliber exist—that the universe includes not just angels but also these extraordinary administrators—should give you profound assurance in the quality of cosmic government. You're part of a system administered by beings whose wisdom and capability far exceed anything Earth has ever produced.

Brilliant Evening Stars ensure that the support you receive from angels is part of a coherent, well-coordinated, expertly administered divine plan. They are the assurance that nothing is left to chance, that high-level oversight maintains quality and consistency, and that the systems designed to help you survive and ascend are functioning as intended.

You will probably never meet a Brilliant Evening Star during the early stages of your ascension. They work at levels too high, on concerns too great.

But their work affects you constantly. The policies they help formulate, the coordination they provide, the administrative decisions they make or advise on—all of this shapes the context in which your guardian angel works, the resources available for your edification, the smooth functioning of the resurrection process, and countless other aspects of your survival and progression.

## The Quality of Cosmic Administration

God doesn't just create angels and hope they figure out how to organize themselves. He creates high administrators—beings of extraordinary wisdom and capability—to ensure that all cosmic functions operate with maximum effectiveness.

This is comforting. You are part of a cosmos where the quality of administration matches the grandeur of divine purposes. Where expertise exists at every level. Where coordination ensures that nothing essential falls through the cracks.

The Brilliant Evening Stars, though remote from your daily experience, are proof that you can trust the system. You can trust that the help you receive from angels is part of a larger, expertly harmonized effort to ensure your survival and facilitate your ascension.

And that trust is not naive optimism. It's justified confidence in a universe where beings of the highest caliber work tirelessly to make divine promises real for every ascending soul.

5

# ARCHANGELS

## MASTERS OF RESURRECTION

AMONG ALL THE ANGELIC ORDERS, ARCHANGELS OCCUPY A UNIQUE AND dramatic role. In addition to high universe administration and leadership, they are the specialists in resurrection—the beings who orchestrate one of the most consequential transitions any mortal ever experiences: the passage from death to renewed life on the mansion worlds.

After you die, an archangel will pronounce your resurrection. In response to that pronouncement, you will be reassembled, rebuilt, and awakened in a new body on a new world, ready to continue a journey that death could not end.

The archangels are masters of this work. They have conducted countless resurrections. They understand the mechanics, the timing, the coordination required. And they perform their duties with unwavering precision.

In our universe, there are almost 800,000 archangels. They organize into divisions and work from their headquarters on a specialized world within the local system. From there, they coordinate resurrection activities throughout the entire local universe.

## THE SLEEP BETWEEN LIVES

When your heart takes its final beat, three entities immediately spring into coordinated action:

*Upon your death, your records, identity specifications, and the morontia entity of the human soul—conjointly evolved by the ministry of mortal mind and the divine spirit—are faithfully conserved by the destiny guardian together with all other values related to your future existence, everything that constitutes you, the real you, except the identity of continuing existence represented by the departing spirit and the actuality of personality.*[1]

Your guardian seraphim takes custody of your identity pattern, that unique template that makes you distinctly you. And your body returns to the elements from which it came. But you? The conscious awareness reading these words right now? You sleep.

Not the sleep of earthly nights, with dreams and restlessness and the slow passage of hours. This sleep is complete unconsciousness—no awareness of time passing, no sense of self, no dreams to occupy the darkness. You could sleep for three days or three years, and you would not know the difference. To you, death feels like closing your eyes in one room and opening them in another, with no perception of the interval between.

How long that interval lasts depends on factors you cannot control. Some wake within days of their death. Others sleep through centuries or millennia, waiting for the dispensational resurrection that will summon entire generations simultaneously. The universe follows patterns and schedules that serve purposes larger than individual convenience. But eventually—certainly, inevitably—your moment comes:

*The instant the pilot light in the human mind disappears, the spirit luminosity which seraphim associate with the presence of the spirit, the attending angel reports in person to the commanding angels,*

## YOUR FIRST MOMENTS

Picture the resurrection halls on the first mansion world. These structures dwarf any building you have ever seen, yet they radiate warmth and welcome. Their architecture speaks of purpose fulfilled, of careful preparation, of spaces designed by beings who understand that form should serve function and that beauty need not conflict with utility.

You open your eyes. The first thing you see is not the hall, though you will notice it soon enough. The first thing you see is a face—familiar yet somehow new, radiant with joy and relief and something that can only be called love made visible.

Your guardian. The seraphim who watched over you through your mortal life, who carried you to this place, who has been waiting for this moment when you would wake and she could finally greet you not as an invisible guide but as a visible companion.

## WHAT YOU ARE NOW

You look down at yourself and see a form that resembles your mortal body but improved, clarified, freed from the limitations imposed by mortal flesh. The form you wear is the truest expression of who you have always been beneath the accidents of genetics and time.

This is called morontia. Not purely material, not yet spiritual, but something between—a body of energy and substance that can touch and be touched, that can feel and express. It may designate personal or impersonal realities, living or nonliving energies. And it will serve you through the long road ahead.

Around you, others are waking. Hundreds of them, perhaps thousands, each attended by their assigned seraphim, each experiencing their own moment of incredulous joy. The hall fills with voices—gasps, laughter, tears, exclamations in languages you have never heard. All of you wake together, bound by nothing except the timing of your resurrection and the shared experience of death overcome.

## The Technique of Survival

The archangels demonstrate something crucial about how the universe operates: even the most spiritual, most transcendent events require technique and execution. Resurrection is not magic. It is not spontaneous. It is not even miraculous in the sense of breaking natural law.

Resurrection is an organized, coordinated process involving multiple orders of beings working according to established procedures. Your survival does not depend on mystical uncertainties or the whims of inscrutable forces. Your survival depends on beings who know exactly what they are doing, who have done it countless times before, who will do it countless times again.

When your moment comes, no one will be improvising. No one will be guessing. No one will be hoping it works out. The systems will operate as designed. Your identity, soul and personality—*you*—will be constructed with precision and perfection. And you will wake.

## The Voice of Victory

In the most fundamental sense, archangels proclaim victory over death every time they conduct a resurrection. Their voices declare that mortality is not the end, that souls can and do survive, that the promise of continued existence is being fulfilled moment by moment across the universe.

This is not theoretical. It is happening right now. On higher worlds throughout this universe and beyond, sleeping souls are awakening.

Former humans begin to understand that everything they feared about death was baseless. Death is not a wall. It is a doorway, and the archangels are the ones who open it from the other side.

Countless times they have witnessed these awakenings. They have seen the shock, the wonder, the overwhelming joy as newly resurrected souls realize that consciousness has continued, that they exist, that the journey goes on.

The archangels never tire of this work. Each resurrection, even after ages of repetition, remains significant because each time, they witness the defeat of death itself. Your resurrection will be routine for them in procedure, but never routine in meaning. Archangels will approach your awakening with the same reverence they brought to the first soul they ever restored.

Every person who has died with even the smallest choice for survival, every soul that formed enough reality to persist beyond the body's dissolution—they have awakened or will awaken. The archangels guarantee this. Their voices are the sounds of that guarantee being fulfilled.

Someday, in the annals of this universe, the fact of your resurrection will be recorded. An archangel will one day stand at that appointed moment, and by the authority vested in these ancient beings, the barriers between death and life will part. Not for the righteous few— for everyone who chose even once to seek something higher. The archangels don't judge worthiness. They execute mercy. And when your moment comes, their voice will be the sound of victory over the last enemy any mortal ever faces.


## Non-Survivors

Archangels coordinate resurrection for mortals into the endless potential of eternal life. But what about those who choose darkness over light, who persist in selfishness and iniquity until the end? Do they go to hell?

Some traditional religions teach eternal conscious torment: fire, suffering, punishment without end. This doctrine has traumatized millions, motivated through fear rather than love, and painted God as vindictive rather than merciful.

It's not true.

There is no hell of eternal torment. No fire, no torture, no endless suffering. God is not a sadist who creates beings for the purpose of punishing them forever. The universe doesn't operate on vengeance. Archangels don't coordinate resurrections while others are dragged to eternal torture. That's fiction, not reality.

What actually happens is simpler and perhaps sadder, though done with nameless patience and endless mercy: those who finally, completely, irreversibly reject survival simply cease to exist. Not punished—erased. Not tortured—annihilated. They become as if they had never been.

This is not common. Survival is the default, not extinction or damnation. Archangels work to resurrect everyone who chooses life. Every possible opportunity for growth is provided. Every chance for repentance is extended. The universe lavishly bends toward mercy.

To actually fail to survive requires persistent, knowing, final rejection of all that is good, true, and beautiful. It requires choosing nothingness over being, isolation over connection, death over life—not once in a moment of weakness, but as a settled, final, unchangeable decision of the will.

Most humans never reach this point. Even if they get close to that, every opportunity to come to the light will be provided in the afterlife. The vast majority of humans survive and are resurrected. Even those who lived in ignorance, who never heard of God or angels—if they sought truth sincerely, if they chose kindness over cruelty, if they loved others and tried to do right—archangels resurrect them. Religious affiliation doesn't determine resurrection eligibility. The content of your character and the direction of your choices do.

Your deceased atheist friend who lived generously? Resurrected. Your Buddhist grandmother who never accepted Christ? Resurrected. Your agnostic neighbor who served others selflessly? Resurrected. Sincere seekers of truth are resurrected regardless of their theology, because God judges hearts, not creeds.

What about the rebels—Lucifer, Satan, and those who followed them? They've been adjudicated. Their rebellion is over. When final judgment comes, they will cease to exist—not tortured for eternity, but removed from reality entirely. Justice without cruelty. Finality without vengeance.

The misguided doctrine of eternal hell served fear-based control, not truth. It made God into a monster and religion into a protection racket. It traumatized children and manipulated adults. It distorted the nature of divine love into something unrecognizable.

You don't need to fear hell. It doesn't exist. What exists is a resurrection system designed to help you survive, archangels assigned to coordinate your new life, angels working to facilitate your growth, and a God who wants you to choose life—and who makes that choice as accessible as possible.

If someone you loved has died, you don't need to wonder if they're being tortured. If they were decent, if they sought truth in whatever way they understood it, if they chose love over hate and kindness over cruelty—they're beginning the next phase of existence.

The worst that happens to a mortal is failure to survive—ceasing to exist. That's sad but not cruel. The person simply ends. No consciousness of loss, no experience of punishment, no awareness of what might have been. Just... nothing.

Most people don't end up there. Most are resurrected. Archangels are masters of resurrection, not damnation. Their entire purpose is facilitating survival, coordinating new life, ensuring that every mortal who wants existence receives it.

Unless you make extraordinary efforts to reject survival completely and finally, you will be resurrected. Not because you're perfect, but because the universe is designed to help imperfect beings become perfect over time.

Fear of hell has motivated enough people for enough centuries. It's time to stop being afraid of a fiction and start living confidently in the truth: archangels will conduct your resurrection, angels will ensure your survival, and you're far more likely to succeed than fail.

That's not permissiveness. That's mercy. And mercy, not fear, should be what motivates growth. Know that you can always and at any time pause and reflect on the goodness of God. This will inevitably bring you to a state where fear finds no footing.

# 6

# TERTIAPHIM AND OMNIAPHIM

## TERTIAPHIM - LOCAL UNIVERSE ANGELS

THE TERTIAPHIM OCCUPY A UNIQUE POSITION IN THE ANGELIC hierarchy. They are liaisons between the local universes and the superuniverse administration. They are bridge-builders, coordinators who ensure smooth communication and cooperation between different levels of cosmic government.

## Created for Coordination

Tertiaphim are created by the Infinite Spirit and certain high superuniverse authorities. They are brought into existence specifically to serve as connectors between realms—to translate, interpret, and correlate between the perfect administration of the superuniverse and the evolving administration of the local universes.

This is necessary work. Local universes are domains of time and space where imperfection still exists, where beings are still learning, where administration is developing rather than complete. Superuniverses operate at a higher level of perfection and efficiency. Bridging these two levels requires specialized skill—and that's exactly what tertiaphim provide.

They ensure that messages from superuniverse authorities reach local universe administrators accurately. They help local universe leaders understand and implement superuniverse directives. They coordinate activities that span both levels of administration. They serve as diplomatic representatives, maintaining harmonious relationships between different orders of beings and different levels of authority.

## Technical and Administrative Ministry

Tertiaphim are not primarily teachers or personal guides. They are specialists in administration, communication, and coordination. They handle technical matters that keep the universe functioning smoothly. They manage information flows. They ensure that protocols are followed. They synchronize schedules and facilitate meetings between high personalities who operate in different domains.

Think of them as the expert staff that makes large organizations function efficiently. They don't set policy, but they ensure that policy is communicated clearly and implemented properly. They don't make major decisions, but they provide the information and coordination that allow others to make informed decisions.

This might sound mundane compared to the dramatic work of the archangels or the profound reflectivity of seconaphim. But it's absolutely essential. Without efficient administration and clear communication, even the best plans would collapse into confusion. The tertiaphim prevent that collapse.

## Your Encounter with Tertiaphim

During your ascension through the local universe, you will occasionally interact with tertiaphim. You might receive information they've coordinated. You might participate in events they've arranged. You might benefit from systems they maintain.

But you probably won't develop deep personal relationships with them the way you will with your guardian seraphim or your superuniverse mentors. They work to keep everything functioning properly so that individuals like you can proceed smoothly through your training.

That doesn't make them less important. It makes them differently important. Every complex system requires both personal ministry and administrative coordination. Tertiaphim provide the coordination. Because of their work, you'll move through your ascension without encountering bureaucratic nightmares, communication breakdowns, or administrative chaos.

The universe works. And the tertiaphim are part of why it works.


## Specialized Service

The tertiaphim teach an important lesson: there is dignity and value in every form of service. Not every angel needs to be a personal savior or a spiritual teacher. Some serve by keeping systems running smoothly, ensuring that communication flows clearly and administration functions efficiently.

This is holy work. It's necessary work. It warrants admiration and appreciation.

When you reach the point in your ascension where you understand how the universe actually operates—where you see the vast coordination required to govern trillions of worlds and facilitate the progression of countless ascending mortals—you'll be grateful for the tertiaphim. You'll recognize that their quiet, technical, administrative work keeps the universe running smoothly.

Angels don't all work in dramatic, visible ways. Some work in the background, handling essential tasks that others rarely notice. The tertiaphim excel at this kind of work. And the universe is better because of them.

# Omniaphim - The Exalted Servants

The omniaphim are the most exclusive angels in creation. They are created solely by the Infinite Spirit and live exclusively in his personal support and in certain specialized functions at the highest levels of universe administration. They do not encounter ascending mortals. They do not work in local universes. They operate on Paradise and in the most elevated circles of cosmic government.

You will never encounter an omniaphim during your mortal life or even during the early stages of your ascension. These exalted beings move in realms far removed from the concerns of evolving mortals. But they deserve mention because they represent the pinnacle of specialized angelic service.

## Exclusive Service

The Infinite Spirit creates omniaphim for specific high purposes. Some are his personal attendants. Some work with the Seven Supreme Executives—the highest administrative authorities next to the Trinity itself. Some fulfill specialized functions in Paradise administration that require unique capabilities.

The exact number and specific duties of omniaphim are not fully revealed. What is clear is that they represent the Infinite Spirit's most capable, most trusted angelic servants. They operate at levels of administration where only the most competent and reliable beings can function.

The omniaphim demonstrate an important principle: not all work is accessible to everyone. Some must be done by specialists at the highest levels. Some functions require capabilities that only the most exalted angels possess.

This doesn't create injustice or inequality. It creates appropriate organization. Just as a complex society requires both frontline workers and high-level administrators, so does the universe require both guardian angels who minister to individuals and exclusive servants who handle the most elevated functions of cosmic government.

The omniaphim fulfill their role with the same dedication that your guardian seraphim fulfills hers. The difference is not in commitment or importance but in sphere of service. Your guardian serves you personally. The omniaphim serve the Infinite Spirit personally and assist in administration at the very top of the cosmic hierarchy.

## Remote but Real

You may never meet an omniaphim. Their work is too far removed from the paths that ascending mortals travel. They operate in dimensions of reality you cannot yet access and handle responsibilities you cannot yet understand.

But they are real. They are working right now, facilitating the highest functions of universe administration, ensuring that the very top levels of cosmic government function with perfect efficiency.

Knowing they exist might elicit a sense of exuberance but also of profound peace. The universe is administered all the way to the top. There are no gaps, no levels where competency is absent, nothing left to chance. From your personal guardian who knows your name and watches over your daily life, all the way to the omniaphim on Paradise in the presence of the Infinite Spirit himself—loving aid is complete, thorough, and expertly provided.

## Universal Care

The omniaphim complete the picture of angelic ministry. They show that angels exist at every level, serving every function, meeting every need. Some are for mortals. Others are for administrators. Some are for the highest cosmic authorities. Others are for technical coordination. Some are for personal guidance. Others are for worship facilitation. There are angels for everything that needs doing.

The universe is thoroughly, completely, expertly served by celestial beings of every order and capacity. Nothing is neglected. No one is forgotten. No function goes unfilled.

That's what the full spectrum of angelic creation accomplishes—from the supernaphim of Paradise to your personal guardian, from the reflective seconaphim to the exclusive omniaphim, angels fill every role, meet every need, and ensure that the vast machinery of divine administration operates flawlessly.

You live in a cosmos where kindness is complete.

7

# THE SERAPHIC ORDERS

Of all the angelic orders, seraphim are the ones you're most likely to encounter, interact with, and be influenced by. As the ministering spirits of the local universe, these angels were created specifically to work with evolving mortals like you. Operating on your world, in your daily life, and throughout your ascension journey, seraphim are neither distant nor theoretical. Present, active, and deeply involved—this describes their relationship to your welfare. Your bond with them will deepen forever:

> *In nature and personality endowment the seraphim are just a trifle ahead of mortal races in the scale of creature existence. Indeed, when you are delivered from the flesh, you become very much like them. On the mansion worlds you will begin to appreciate the seraphim, on the constellation spheres to enjoy them, while on Salvington they will share their places of rest and worship with you. Throughout the whole morontia and subsequent spirit ascent, your fraternity with the seraphim will be ideal; your companionship will be superb.*[1]

Our universe contains many billions of seraphim. They are organized into divisions, legions, companies, battalions, and armies. Each has specific assignments, specific capabilities, and specific purposes. They fall into various categories based on their function and the scope of their work.

## SUPREME SERAPHIM

Seraphim of the supreme order are the highest ranking in the local universe. Seven specialized corps comprise this order:

**The Sons' Attendants** serve the planetary missions of the Divine Sons, who are accompanied

> *by this high and experienced order of seraphim, who are devoted to organizing and administering the special work connected with the termination of one planetary dispensation and the inauguration of a new age. They are especially trained to meet the difficulties and to cope with the emergencies associated with the bestowals of the Sons of God for the advancement of the children of time.*[2]

**The Court Advisers** work with the judicial system of the universe, providing insight and guidance in matters requiring angelic perspective.

> *It is not the purpose of such tribunals to determine punitive sentences but rather to adjudicate honest differences of opinion and to decree the everlasting survival of ascending mortals. Herein lies the duty of the court advisers: to see that all charges against mortal creatures are stated in justice and adjudicated in mercy.*[3]

**Universe Orientators** help newly created beings and ascending mortals understand the universe—its structure, its purposes, its opportunities. As teachers of cosmic geography and divine administration, these orientators ensure teaching remains effective, accurate, and appropriate for students at every level of development.

> *It is the task of the universe orientators to facilitate the passage of the ascending pilgrims from the attained to the unattained level of*

*universe service, to help these pilgrims in making those kaleidoscopic adjustments in the comprehension of meanings and values inherent in the realization that a first stage spirit being stands, not at the end and climax of the local universe morontia ascent, but rather at the very bottom of the long ladder of spiritual ascent to the Universal Father on Paradise.*[4]

**The Teaching Counselors** coordinate educational programs throughout the local universe. They ensure that teaching remains effective, accurate, and appropriate for students at every level of development.

*These angels are the invaluable assistants of the spiritual teaching corps of the universe.*[5]

**Directors of Assignment** facilitate the placement of seraphim in their various roles. When guardian angels are needed on a newly settled world, these directors make the assignments. When seraphim complete one phase of duty and are ready for new challenges, these directors determine their next postings.

*These angels preside over all seraphic assemblies pertaining to the line of duty or the call to worship.*[6]

**The Recorders** maintain the records of the local universe. They preserve significant events and important decisions. Nothing of value is lost because these beings faithfully record it.

*Many of these high angels were born with their gifts fully developed; others have qualified for their positions of trust and responsibility by diligent application to study and faithful performance of similar duties while attached to lower or less responsible orders.*[7]

**Unattached Ministers** labor as a reserve force, ready to handle emergencies or special assignments that don't fit into the regular categories of seraphic ministry.

*Large numbers of unattached seraphim of the supreme order are self-directed servers on the architectural spheres and on the inhabited planets.*[8]

The supreme seraphim operate at the highest levels of local universe administration. They maintain the systems, coordinate the resources, and ensure the smooth operation of everything that makes mortal survival and progression viable.

## SUPERIOR SERAPHIM

*Superior seraphim receive their name, not because they are in any sense qualitatively superior to other orders of angels, but because they are in charge of the higher activities of a universe.*[9]

Superior seraphim work more directly in facilitating mortal ascension. Seven groups comprise this order:

**The Intelligence Corps** gather and distribute information throughout the local universe, serving as the communication network that keeps worlds connected and administrators informed.

*These seraphim belong to the personal staff of Gabriel, the Bright and Morning Star. They range the universe gathering the information of the realms for his guidance.*[10]

**The Voices of Mercy** proclaim divine compassion throughout the universe. They ensure that mercy is not just a concept but an active, ongoing reality in the treatment of all beings.

*Mercy is the keynote of seraphic service and angelic ministry. They are the inspired leaders who foster the higher impulses and holier emotions of men and angels.*[11]

**Spirit Coordinators** help synchronize the various spiritual influences that work on mortal minds. They ensure that these influences work harmoniously rather than in conflict.

> *While their tasks are essentially spiritual and therefore beyond the real understanding of human minds, these seraphim instruct regarding newly attained capacities of the mind of the spirit.*[12]

**Assistant Teachers** support the educational work of the universe, serving as aides to the more senior teaching personalities and helping to deliver instruction to ascending mortals.

> *They are also individually connected with the extensive educational enterprises of the local universe. A marvelous corps of this order of seraphim functions on Earth for the purpose of fostering and furthering the cause of truth and righteousness.*[13]

**The Transporters** move beings to and from the capital of this universe.

> *The process of being enseraphimed is not unlike the experience of death or sleep except that there is an automatic time element in the transit slumber. You are consciously unconscious during seraphic rest. When enseraphimed, you go to sleep for a specified time, and you will awake at the designated moment. You are not directly aware of the passing of time.*[14]

**The Recorders** are concerned with the reception, filing, and redispatch of the records of the universe.

> *Their work is of a high order, being so multicircuited that 144,000 messages can simultaneously traverse the same lines of energy.*[15]

**The Reserves** stand ready for special assignments or emergency service wherever needed.

*A local universe is fully provided with adequate means of intercommunication, but there is always a residue of messages which requires dispatch by personal messengers.*[16]

---

Superior seraphim work closer to the lives of individual mortals than supreme seraphim do. Their ministry has direct impact on your experience, even if you're not consciously aware of their presence.

## SUPERVISOR SERAPHIM

Supervisor seraphim oversee specific types of functions across the constellations. Seven divisions structure this order:

**Supervising Assistants** are concerned with the unification and stabilization of a whole constellation.

*They are assigned to the collective work of the Constellation Fathers, and they are the ever-efficient helpers of the Most Highs.*[17]

**Law Forecasters** help interpret and apply universe law, in addition to ensuring that regulations are understood correctly and applied consistently.

*The intellectual foundation of justice is law, and in a local universe law originates in the legislative assemblies of the constellations. These deliberative bodies codify and formally promulgate basic laws designed to afford the greatest possible co-ordination of a whole constellation consistent with the fixed policy of noninfringement of the moral free will of personal creatures.*

*Even mortal man may contribute to the evolution of universe law, for these very seraphim do faithfully and fully portray the true longings of the inner man, the evolving soul of the material mortal on the worlds of space.*[18]

**Social Architects** design and facilitate social structures that promote healthy relationships and community development on worlds throughout the universe.

*These are the angels who seek to divest the associations of intelligent beings of all artificiality while endeavoring to facilitate the interassociation of will creatures on a basis of real self-understanding and genuine mutual appreciation.*[19]

**Ethical Sensitizers** help beings develop moral awareness and ethical judgment. They don't impose rules; they help individuals and societies recognize what's right and good.

*It is the mission of these seraphim to foster and to promote the growth of creature appreciation of the morality of interpersonal relationships, for such is the seed and secret of the continued and purposeful growth of society and government, human or superhuman.*[20]

**The Transporters** at this level carry beings to and from the various constellation headquarters.

**The Recorders** maintain archives at the constellation level, preserving information about entire worlds and systems rather than just individuals.

**The Reserves** provide specialized backup for any supervisor function that requires additional resources.

## ADMINISTRATOR SERAPHIM

Administrator seraphim work at the system level, managing the practical details of universe governance which oversees up to 1,000 worlds. They organize into seven types:

**Administrative Assistants** support the System Sovereigns who govern individual systems of inhabited worlds.

> *They are invaluable aids in the execution of the intricate details of the executive work of the system headquarters. They also serve as the personal agents of the system rulers, journeying back and forth in large numbers to the various transition worlds and to the inhabited planets, executing many commissions for the welfare of the system and in the physical and biologic interests of its inhabited worlds.*[21]

**Justice Guides** assist in the administration of fair and merciful justice throughout the system.

> *These are the angels who present the summary of evidence concerning the eternal welfare of men and angels when such matters come up for adjudication in the tribunals of a system or a planet.*
>
> *The defense of all cases of doubtful survival is prepared by these seraphim, who have a perfect understanding of all the details of every feature of every count in the indictments drawn by the administrators of universe justice.*[22]

**Interpreters of Cosmic Citizenship** help new mansion world graduates enjoying the fruits of their labor by instructing them regarding their rights and responsibilities as citizens of the local universe.

> *When ascending mortals have completed the mansion world training, the first student apprenticeship in the universe career, they are permitted to enjoy the transient satisfactions of relative maturity—citizenship on the system capital.*
>
> *Ever and anon there is a pause in the Paradise ascent, a short breathing spell, during which universe horizons stand still, creature status is stationary, and the personality tastes the sweetness of goal fulfillment.*[23]

**Quickeners of Morality** stimulate ethical awareness and moral development in individuals and societies.

> *On the mansion worlds you begin to learn self-government for the benefit of all concerned. Your mind learns cooperation, learns how to plan with other and wiser beings. On the system headquarters the seraphic teachers will further quicken your appreciation of cosmic morality—of the interactions of liberty and loyalty.*[24]

**The Transporters** manage transport at the system level.

> *Seldom does a day pass in which a transport seraphim does not deposit some student visitor or some other traveler of spirit or semi-spirit nature on the shores of Earth. These very space traversers will sometime carry you to and from the various worlds of the system headquarters group, and when you have finished the assignment, they will carry you forward.*[25]

**The Recorders** maintain system archives.

> *The temple of records on a system capital is a unique structure, one third material, constructed of luminous metals and crystals; one third fabricated of the liaison of spiritual and material energy but beyond the range of mortal vision; and one third spiritual.*[26]

**The Reserves** stand ready for special administrative assignments.

> *The reserve corps of administrator seraphim on the system capital spend much of their waiting time in visiting, as spirit companions, with the newly arrived ascending mortals from the various worlds of the system.*

> *One of the delights of your sojourn here will be to talk and visit with these much-traveled and many-experienced seraphim of the waiting reserve corps. Mortal forms are there so modified and human ranges*

*of light reaction so extended that all are able to enjoy mutual recognition and sympathetic personality understanding.*[27]

## UNREVEALED ANGELS

You now know the nine orders of angels directly involved in human development and planetary administration.

But these represent only a fraction of angelic populations. Numerous other orders function throughout creation—orders that have no direct connection to human evolution and are therefore not revealed to us in detail:

> *There serve in the local universe six other orders of related beings, the unrevealed angels, who are not in any specific manner connected with those universe activities pertaining to the Paradise ascent of evolutionary mortals. These six groups of angelic associates are never called seraphim, neither are they referred to as ministering spirits.*
>
> *These personalities are wholly occupied with the administrative and other universe affairs, engagements which are in no way related to man's progressive career of spiritual ascent and perfection attainment.*[28]

This is both humbling and awe-inspiring. The universe is far more complex, populated, and organized than we can currently comprehend. The angels we've discussed in this book—the ones who guide us, protect us, and facilitate our eternal journey—are just the beginning. We are surrounded by celestial administrators and specialists engaged in cosmic work we cannot yet imagine.

For now, we focus on what concerns us: the angels whose mission is our survival, growth, and ultimate perfection. But knowing there are countless others reminds us that we are part of something infinitely greater than ourselves.

These seraphic orders—Supreme, Superior, Supervisor, Administrator, and Unrevealed—work at universe, constellation, and system levels. Their ministry might seem distant, but don't mistake distance for irrelevance. They maintain the infrastructure of ascension.

Yet there are seraphim who work much closer to home. Angels who don't just maintain cosmic systems but who serve directly as aids to mortals—on your world, in your society, throughout your daily life. But before we meet them, let's discover the magnificent abodes of these heavenly helpers.

8

# THE ANGELIC HOME WORLDS

Just as universal order is real, so are the places angels call home. Angels are not homeless wanderers drifting through space. They have worlds of their own—specific planets designed for their training, rest, recreation, and administration. These angelic home worlds exist throughout the universe, from Paradise itself to the headquarters of local systems, and each serves as a base of operations for particular orders of ministering spirits.

Understanding where angels live when they're not ministering to mortals reveals another dimension of their reality. They are citizens of actual worlds, beings with homes and communities, not just abstract spiritual presences. They gather, they train, they plan, they play—and they do all of this on physical worlds created specifically for their needs.

## PARADISE

Primary supernaphim, the highest order of angels, dwell on Paradise itself.

*They do not function extensively outside Paradise, though they do participate in the various millennial gatherings and group reunions of the central universe. They also go forth as special messengers of the Deities.* [1]

For these angels, Paradise is not just a workplace—it's their home. They know the eternal Isle. They are permanent residents of the center of all things:

*Paradise is the eternal center of the universe of universes and the abiding place of the Universal Father, the Eternal Son, the Infinite Spirit, and their divine co-ordinates and associates. This central Isle is the most gigantic organized body of cosmic reality in all the master universe.*

*Paradise is a material sphere as well as a spiritual abode. All of the intelligent creation of the Universal Father is domiciled on material abodes; hence must the absolute controlling center also be material, literal. And again it should be reiterated that spirit things and spiritual beings are real.*

*The material beauty of Paradise consists in the magnificence of its physical perfection; the grandeur of the Isle of God is exhibited in the superb intellectual accomplishments and mind development of its inhabitants; the glory of the central Isle is shown forth in the infinite endowment of divine spirit personality—the light of life.*

*But the depths of the spiritual beauty and the wonders of this magnificent ensemble are utterly beyond the comprehension of the finite mind of material creatures. The glory and spiritual splendor of the divine abode are impossible of mortal comprehension. And Paradise is from eternity; there are neither records nor traditions respecting the origin of this nuclear Isle of Light and Life.* [2]

## SERAPHINGTON

*Between the central Isle of Paradise and the innermost of the Havona planetary circuits there are situated in space three lesser circuits of special spheres. These three seven-world circuits of the Father, the Son, and the Spirit are spheres of unexcelled grandeur and unimagined glory. Even their material or physical construction is of an order unrevealed to you. All twenty-one are enormous spheres, and each group of seven is differently eternalized.[3]*

The most important of these worlds is called Seraphington, the destiny sphere of all ministering orders of the angelic hosts, functioning as the threshold to Paradise and Deity attainment. And it is significant to an even broader range of spirit beings:

*There also serve in the central and outlying universes many orders of superb spirits who are not ministering spirits. All these spirit workers in all levels and realms of universe activities look upon Seraphington as their Paradise home.[4]*

Here, the seraphic guardians eventually achieve the seven circles of seraphic light, achieving transformations that qualify them for eternal service at the highest levels. No seraphim who attains Seraphington has ever fallen. Sin finds no response in the heart of a seraphim of completion. They have achieved a level of perfection that makes sin impossible.

## HAVONA

The billion perfect worlds of Havona are home to secondary supernaphim. These superangels are native to the central universe, created specifically to serve in that realm. They live on the Havona spheres, minister to ascending pilgrims passing through, and maintain the perfect administration of the perfect worlds.

For secondary supernaphim, Havona represents the ideal environment—worlds without imperfection, without error, without the difficulties that characterize the evolutionary realms. They serve in paradisiacal conditions, ministering to beings who are close to achieving Paradise itself.

> *The perfect and divine universe occupies the center of all creation; it is the eternal core around which the vast creations of time and space revolve. It is of enormous dimensions and almost unbelievable mass and consists of one billion spheres of unimagined beauty and superb grandeur, but the true magnitude of this vast creation is really beyond the understanding grasp of the human mind.*
>
> *This is the one and only settled, perfect, and established aggregation of worlds. This is a wholly created and perfect universe; it is not an evolutionary development.*
>
> *This is the eternal core of perfection, about which swirls that endless procession of universes which constitute the tremendous evolutionary experiment, the audacious adventure of the Sons of God, who aspire to duplicate in time and to reproduce in space the pattern universe, the ideal of divine completeness, supreme finality, ultimate reality, and eternal perfection.*[5]

## EVENING STAR WORLDS

The Brilliant Evening Stars maintain their own headquarters worlds within the local universe. These are administrative centers where these high beings harmonize their liaison work between different levels of universe government.

These worlds are meeting places where Brilliant Evening Stars confer with universe administrators, train for their advisory roles, and plan their coordination activities. They are sophisticated centers of government where policies affecting entire constellations and systems are discussed and implemented.

*The sixth group of seven Salvington worlds and their forty-two tribu-
tary satellites are assigned to the administration of the Brilliant
Evening Stars. The seven primary worlds are presided over by the
created orders of these superangels, while the tributary satellites are
administered by ascendant Evening Stars.*[6]

## SALVINGTON

Salvington, the headquarters of the local universe, serves as home to
countless orders of beings, including supreme seraphim and other
high angelic orders. But surrounding Salvington are 490 satellites,
and many of these serve specific functions related to angelic training
and administration.

*These headquarters worlds are among the magnificent realms of the
universe; the seraphic estates are characterized by both beauty and
vastness. Here each seraphim has a real home, and home means the
domicile of two seraphim; they live in pairs.*[7]

These satellite worlds include training spheres where newly created
seraphim learn their roles, administrative centers where angelic policies are coordinated, and rest spheres where angels can recuperate
between assignments. Each satellite has specific purposes, and they
travel between them regularly as their duties require.

## EDENTIA

*The government of your constellation is situated in a cluster of 771
architectural spheres, the centermost and largest of which is Edentia,
the seat of the administration of the Constellation Fathers.*[8]

Edentia, the headquarters of the constellation, is surrounded by 70
architectural satellites, and several of these function as angelic worlds.
Here supervisor seraphim and other constellation-level angels maintain their base of operations.

The constellation spheres are breathtakingly beautiful—gardens, artistic centers, and training facilities that showcase the highest achievements of architectural design.





## Jerusem

The headquarters of the local system, Jerusem, is orbited by seven major satellites and numerous minor worlds, many of which function as angelic bases. Administrator seraphim, transition ministers preparing for mansion world duties, and other orders of local system angels all maintain facilities on these worlds.

*The light rays do not seem to come from one place; they just sift out of the sky, emanating equally from all space directions. This light is very similar to natural sunlight except that it contains very much less heat.*

*Jerusem receives faint light from several near-by suns—a sort of brilliant starlight. It is indeed a foretaste of paradisiacal glory and grandeur.*[11]

The mansion worlds themselves, while primarily designed for ascending mortals, also house extensive seraphic populations. Transition ministers live on these worlds permanently, providing continuous ministry to the ascending mortals who pass through them. These angels have their own dwellings, their own community life, and their own administrative structures.

## ANGELIC TRAINING WORLDS

Throughout the local universe, specific worlds are dedicated to angelic training. Newly created seraphim spend considerable time on these spheres learning the technical skills required for their assignments. They study the nature of ascending mortals, the structure of universe government, the principles of energy manipulation, and countless other subjects.

These training worlds are not merely schools. They are complete societies where young seraphim develop friendships, form working partnerships (especially with their cherubim companions), and prepare for the long careers ahead of them. The education is thorough, practical, and designed to produce angels capable of handling the complex challenges of universe existence.

## REST AND RECREATION

Angels need rest. While they don't experience physical exhaustion in the same way mortals do, they do experience something like mental or spiritual fatigue. Throughout the universe, specific realms exist where angels can retreat for recuperation and recreation.

These rest zones offer beauty, peace, and opportunities for activities that refresh their spirits. Angels gather there to share experiences, renew friendships with former associates, and prepare mentally and spiritually for new assignments. The rest is sublime, and they return from these retreats genuinely refreshed and ready for renewed service.

---

The existence of angelic home worlds proves that angels are not abstract spirits floating in undefined space. They are concrete beings with actual residences, real communities, and physical locations they call home.

When a guardian seraphim is assigned a period of rest, she goes somewhere. She has living quarters on a world orbiting other worlds. She gathers with other angels, shares experiences. She plays and participates in angelic society. She is not just out there vaguely—she is specifically somewhere, on an actual world, living an actual life.

This should make angels more real to you. They are not mere concepts or forces. They are persons with homes, with communities, with lives that extend beyond their ministry to you. Understanding this adds depth to your appreciation of who they are and what they sacrifice when they dedicate centuries or millennia to guiding a single ascending mortal through the universe.

Angels have worlds. Beautiful worlds. Sophisticated worlds. Worlds designed specifically for their natures and needs. And someday, when you are far enough in your ascension, you will see these places. The mansion worlds, the constellation realms, even the universe headquarters spheres—these aren't fictional places. They're destinations on your journey. Real worlds where you'll walk, learn, and grow.

9

---

# THE PLANETARY SERAPHIM

*These angelic orders are projected at the time of planning for the evolution of mortal will creatures. Seraphim are still being periodically created; our universe is still in the making. The Universe Mother Spirit never ceases creative activity in a growing and perfecting universe.*[1]

YOU'VE NOW BEEN TOLD OF THE ORGANIZATIONAL HEIGHTS AND THE glorious worlds of the daughters of the Infinite Spirit. Now meet the angels who work directly with you.

These are the seraphic aids to mortals—angels specifically assigned to planetary populations, to human societies, and to individual souls making their way through material existence. They don't work in distant cosmic headquarters. They work here, on Earth, among humanity. And their ministry touches your life in ways both subtle and profound.

## Planetary Helpers

Planetary helpers work directly on inhabited worlds like Earth. They are primarily assigned to the serve the Planetary Adams, the biologic uplifters of the material races on the evolutionary worlds.

*The ministering work of angels becomes of increasing interest as it nears the inhabited worlds, as it nears the actual problems faced by the men and women of time who are preparing themselves for the attempt to attain the goal of eternity.*[2]

They organize into twelve groups:

**The Voices of the Garden** once ministered in the Garden of Eden.

*When the planetary course of human evolution is attaining its highest biologic level, there always appear the Material Sons and Daughters, the Adams and Eves, to augment the further evolution of the races by an actual contribution of their superior life plasm. The planetary headquarters of such an Adam and Eve is usually denominated the Garden of Eden, and their personal seraphim are often known as the "voices of the Garden."*[3]

**The Spirits of Brotherhood** work to foster unity, cooperation, and mutual respect among individuals, groups, and nations. They encourage whatever helps people recognize their kinship and work together.

*It should be apparent that, when an Adam and Eve arrive on an evolutionary world, the task of achieving racial harmony and social cooperation among its diverse races is one of considerable proportions.*

*Seldom do these races of different colors and varied natures take kindly to the plan of human brotherhood. These primitive men only come to realize the wisdom of peaceful interassociation as a result of ripened human experience and through the faithful ministry of the seraphic spirits of brotherhood.*[4]

**The Souls of Peace** labor constantly to promote peaceful resolution of conflicts. They don't prevent violence, but they work tirelessly to create conditions in which peace will eventually manifest.

*The early millenniums of the upward strivings of evolutionary men are marked by many a struggle. Peace is not the natural state of the material realms. The worlds first realize "peace on earth and good will among men" through the ministry of the seraphic souls of peace.*

*In the more advanced epochs of planetary evolution these seraphim are instrumental in supplanting the atonement idea by the concept of divine attunement as a philosophy of mortal survival.[5]*

**The Spirits of Trust** encourage honesty, reliability, and trustworthiness in human relationships. They foster qualities conducive to stable societies and meaningful relationships.

*Suspicion is the inherent reaction of primitive men; the survival struggles of the early ages do not naturally breed trust. Trust is a new human acquisition brought about by the ministry of these planetary seraphim of the Adamic regime.*

*In the more advanced planetary ages these seraphim enhance man's appreciation of the truth that uncertainty is the secret of contented continuity. They help the mortal philosophers to realize that, when ignorance is essential to success, it would be a colossal blunder for the creature to know the future.*

*They heighten man's taste for the sweetness of uncertainty, for the romance and charm of the indefinite and unknown future.[6]*

**The Transporters** serve individual worlds, moving enseraphimed beings between planets and system headquarters. A large number are stationed on Earth, operating transport between here and Jerusem. Most beings they carry are in transit, stopping over briefly before continuing to their destination.

*In observing a transport seraphim being made ready to receive a passenger for interplanetary transit, there may be seen what are apparently double sets of wings extending from the head to the foot of the angel. In reality these wings are energy insulators—friction shields.*

*The transport seraphim moves into a horizontal position immediately above the universe energy pole of the planet. While the energy shields are wide open, the personality is skillfully deposited directly on top of the transport angel.*

*Then both the upper and lower pairs of shields are carefully closed and adjusted. And now a strange metamorphosis begins as the seraphim is made ready to swing into the energy currents of the universe circuits. To outward appearance the seraphim grows pointed at both extremities and becomes so enshrouded in a queer light of amber hue that very soon it is impossible to distinguish the enseraphimed personality.*

*When all is in readiness for departure, the chief of transport makes the proper inspection of the carriage of life, carries out the routine tests to ascertain whether or not the angel is properly encircuited, and then announces that the traveler is properly enseraphimed, that the energies are adjusted, that the angel is insulated, and that everything is in readiness for the departing flash. By this time the transport seraphim has become an almost transparent, vibrating, torpedo-shaped outline of glistening luminosity.*

*Now the transport dispatcher of the realm summons the auxiliary batteries of the living energy transmitters, usually one thousand in number; as he announces the destination of the transport, he reaches out and touches the near point of the seraphic carriage, which shoots forward with lightning-like speed, leaving a trail of celestial luminosity as far as the planetary atmospheric investment extends. In less than ten minutes the marvelous spectacle will be lost even to reinforced seraphic vision.*[7]

**The Recorders** on evolving planets maintain detailed records of significant events related to and concerning the universe government.

**The Reserves** stand ready to handle planetary emergencies or special needs.

## Masters of Planetary Supervision

Beyond the regular orders of seraphim who minister to individual mortals and manage routine planetary functions, there exists a specialized group of twelve seraphic corps assigned specifically to Earth's advancement and protection. These elite seraphim of Paradise attainment supervise the largest-scale angelic work affecting human civilization.

These twelve corps form a specialized cabinet dedicated to guiding planetary development. Each focuses on a specific aspect of human civilization, and together they ensure that Earth continues developing toward its ultimate spiritual destiny.

**Civilization Architects:** Three corps shape the broad trajectory of human progress.

*The Epochal Angels* ensure current events fit into the larger pattern of each age, coordinating how contemporary affairs contribute to long-term planetary development. *The Progress Angels* foster inherent progressive trends, constantly moving civilization toward what it ought to become rather than accepting what it currently is. *The Angels of the Future* forecast coming ages and design frameworks for successive eras, serving as the architects of tomorrow.

**Institutional Guardians:** Four corps focus on humanity's foundational structures.

*The Religious Guardians* preserve spiritual ideals and help translate moral values across generations. *The Angels of Nation Life* influence political developments and international relations, working behind the scenes to advance planetary welfare. *The Angels of the Races* foster cooperation among Earth's diverse populations while honoring each group's unique contributions. *The Home Seraphim* preserve and strengthen the family as civilization's fundamental building block.

**Human Development Specialists:** Four more corps advance specific dimensions of human welfare.

*The Angels of Enlightenment* foster education at every level, advancing both intellectual understanding and moral development. *The Angels of Health* assist medical professionals, researchers, and public health agencies in promoting physical wellbeing. *The Angels of Industry* encourage economic development and improved working conditions that serve human welfare rather than merely generating profit. *The Angels of Diversion* promote healthy recreation, humor, and rest, maintaining the balance between work and play.

**Coordination Ministry:** The twelfth corps, the *Angels of Superhuman Ministry*, minister to other celestial beings on Earth—the angels who serve angels, ensuring all superhuman personalities working on the planet receive needed support.

---

*None of these angelic groups exercise direct or arbitrary control over the domains of their assignment. They cannot fully control the affairs of their respective realms of action, but they can and do so manipulate planetary conditions and so associate circumstances as favorably to influence the spheres of human activity to which they are attached.*[8]

They function as clearinghouses for ideas, helping the best human concepts gain traction and spread. They intensify higher ideals that have already emerged in human minds.

Most importantly, they maintain the reserve corps of destiny—special humans scattered across the planet who can be mobilized in emergencies to prevent evolutionary breakdown. These reservists serve as insurance against disaster, so that no matter what chaos erupts, the essential development of civilization will continue.

The master seraphim disagree among themselves about policies and methods, just as human leaders do. But their disagreements are resolved through established procedures, and their unified commitment to planetary advancement never wavers. They have toiled on Earth faithfully through rebellion, default, and countless human catastrophes—and they will continue serving until this troubled world finally achieves the enlightened status it was always meant to reach.


## TRANSITION MINISTERS

Transition ministers work specifically with ascending mortals after death, helping them navigate the mansion worlds and early stages of post-mortal existence. They organize into seven groups:

**Seraphic Evangels** proclaim the gospel of eternal progression to newly resurrected mortals, helping them understand the journey ahead and choose between several options.

> *You are not given unrestricted choice as to your future course; but you may choose within the limits of that which the transition ministers and their superiors wisely determine to be most suitable for your future spirit attainment. The spirit world is governed on the principle of respecting your freewill choice provided the course you may choose is not detrimental to you or injurious to your fellows.*[9]

**Racial Interpreters** help mortals from different planetary backgrounds understand and appreciate each other, fostering unity amid diversity.

**Mind Planners** facilitate educational programs on the mansion worlds, designing curricula that address the specific needs of each ascending mortal.

> *They are the psychologists of the first heaven. Here you are face to face with true friends and understanding counselors, angels who are really able to help you "to see yourself as others see you" and "to know yourself as angels know you."*[10]

**Morontia Counselors** provide personal guidance to ascending mortals as they adjust to semi-spirit existence (that phase of reality between material and spiritual) and navigate the challenges of early ascension.

> *They are the teachers of those who seek insight into the experiential unity of divergent life levels, those who are attempting the integration of meanings and the unification of values. This is the function of philosophy in mortal life, of mota on the morontia spheres. Mota is more than a superior philosophy; it is to philosophy as two eyes are to one; it has a stereoscopic effect on meanings and values. Material man sees the universe, as it were, with but one eye—flat. Mansion world students achieve cosmic perspective—depth—by superimposing the perceptions of the morontia life upon the perceptions of the physical life.* [11]

**Technicians** helps individuals adjust to the new and comparatively strange environment of semi-spirit life.

> *Life on the transition worlds entails real contact with the energies and materials of both the physical and morontia levels and to a certain extent with spiritual realities. Ascenders must acclimatize to every new morontia level, and in all of this they are greatly helped by the seraphic technicians.* [12]

**Recorder-Teachers** both maintain records and provide instruction, combining archival work with educational opportunity.

> *These seraphim are the recorders of the borderland transactions of the spiritual and the physical, of the relationships of men and angels. There is an artistry in the intelligent assembly and coordination of related data. Some day they will teach you to seek truth as well as fact, to expand your soul as well as your mind. Even now you should learn to water the garden of your heart as well as to seek for the dry sands of knowledge.* [13]

**Ministering Reserves** stand ready to assist in any aspect of transition ministry that requires additional resources.

> *Angels take delight in service and, when unassigned, often minister as volunteers. The soul of many an ascending mortal has for the first time been kindled by the divine fire of the will-to-service through personal friendship with the volunteer servers of the seraphic reserves. From them you will learn to let pressure develop stability and certainty; to be faithful and earnest and, withal, cheerful; to accept challenges without complaint and to face difficulties and uncertainties without fear.*
>
> *They will ask: If you fail, will you rise indomitably to try anew? If you succeed, will you maintain a well-balanced poise—a stabilized and spiritualized attitude—throughout every effort in the long struggle to break the fetters of material inertia, to attain the freedom of spirit existence?*
>
> *They will point out that sometimes your most disappointing disappointments have become your greatest blessings. Sometimes the planting of a seed necessitates its death, the death of your fondest hopes, before it can be reborn to bear the fruits of new life and new opportunity. You will learn that you increase your burdens and decrease the likelihood of success by taking yourself too seriously.*[14]

When you wake up after your death, these beings of light will be there. They will help you adjust, guide your early training, and ensure that you successfully navigate the transition from material mortal to morontia being.

## THE REALITY OF SERAPHIC MINISTRY

This catalog of seraphic orders might seem overwhelming. How can you possibly relate to such a vast and complex organization?

You don't have to understand the entire system. You just need to know that the system exists, that it's comprehensive, and that somewhere within it, specific angels are assigned to minister to you personally.

Your guardian knows you. The planetary helpers influence your world. The transition ministers wait to guide you after death. The administrator, supervisor, superior, and supreme seraphim all work to maintain the systems that ensure your survival and ascension.

You are surrounded by intelligent, capable, devoted angels who exist specifically to help you survive, grow, and eventually reach Paradise. This is the actual structure of angelic ministry in the universe.

The seraphim are real. They are here. And they are working on your behalf right now.

10

# GUARDIAN ANGELS

## YOUR PERSONAL COMPANIONS

ANGELS POSSESS DISTINCT PERSONALITY CHARACTERISTICS THAT EXPRESS as masculine or feminine qualities. Seraphim are traditionally regarded with the feminine pronoun, for they are the daughters of the local universe Mother Spirit, in contrast to the Sons of God. Interestingly, seraphim work in complementary pairs—one more aggressive and dynamic, the other more retiring and contemplative—creating a balanced polarity essential to their ministry. Your guardian seraphim is a fully conscious, intelligent being with a name, a personality, preferences, and a specific assignment: you.

From the moment you became capable of making your first true moral choice, a seraphic guardian stepped forward. This angel had been watching, waiting, assessing. And when that moment came, when you made that first real decision between right and wrong, your guardian made a choice too. She claimed you.

## THE ASSIGNMENT

Guardian angels are not randomly distributed. The assignment of a seraphim to an individual mortal is a deliberate act based on achievement, demonstrated ability, and the ascending mortal's potential for eternal survival. Not every human receives a personal guardian immediately. Some mortals share guardians in groups until they exhibit sufficient spiritual receptivity and survival potential to warrant individual attention. But once you receive your personal guardian, that relationship becomes unbreakable.

Your seraphim knows you completely. She knows what you're capable of becoming, even when you can't see it yourself. She has watched you at your worst and cheered you at your best. She has witnessed every kindness you thought no one noticed and every quiet moment of courage.

And she never judges you. Her mission is not to condemn but to foster—to help you survive, to grow, to choose the eternal path.

## HER MINISTRY

The popular image of guardian angels is sentimental and vague: a protective presence that keeps you from harm. The reality is far more specific and infinitely more fascinating.

Your seraphim cannot force you to make right choices, or prevent you from making wrong ones. Your decisions are yours alone.

What she *can* do is work behind the scenes in ways you rarely detect. Her primary function is coordination:

> *One of the most important things a destiny guardian does for her mortal subject is to effect a personal coordination of the numerous impersonal spirit influences which indwell, surround, and impinge upon the mind and soul of the evolving material creature. In the ministry of the guarding angel all of these influences are more or less unified and made more nearly appreciable by the expanding moral nature of the evolving human personality.*[1]

She cannot read your thoughts—that intimate realm belongs to you and God alone. But she perceives your spiritual state, your moral trajectory, the direction of your choices.

Your guardian works constantly with the fragment of God that indwells your mind. While the indwelling spirit works *within* your consciousness, the seraphim works *around* you. Together, they form an unparalleled team dedicated to your survival and development.

Picture a moment of moral choice. You're tempted to lie, to betray a trust, to take the wrong path. Your guardian cannot stop you—but she can make the pull of conscience stronger, the voice of your better self louder. She coordinates the influences already present in your mind, harmonizing them so that wisdom has a better chance against temptation. The choice remains yours. But the battlefield is less chaotic, the right path clearer.

She also sponsors the recording of the undertaking. This record becomes essential at death, when your identity must be reconstructed in the worlds on high.


## When Death Comes

Death is not what you think it is. It's not an ending, not a journey into the unknown, not a leap of faith into darkness. It's a planned transition, executed with precision by beings who know exactly what they're doing.

When your heart beats its last and your lungs draw their final breath, your guardian angel is already in motion. She has been preparing for this moment since the day she claimed you. She knows what to do. This is not improvisation—this is practiced procedure.

At the instant of death, she captures your identity. Everything that makes you *you*—your memories, your personality, your character, your relationships, your accumulated wisdom—is preserved with perfect fidelity. Nothing essential is lost. Not your sense of humor. Not your love for those you're leaving behind. Not the lessons you learned or the person you became. You are fully and completely retained.

You won't experience this preservation. Death brings immediate unconsciousness—not frightening, not painful, simply the cessation of material awareness. You close your eyes on this world unaware of the sophisticated spiritual technology being employed to secure your identity for transport.

Your guardian carries you across vast distances to the first of many worlds where you will continue your existence. You experience none of this journey. For you, there is only the closing of eyes here and the opening of eyes there—two moments that feel consecutive though they are separated by the time required for your transport and reconstruction.

When you awaken, you awaken in a body suited to your new environment. Not your material body—that stays behind, returned to the elements it came from. You wake in a form that is both physical and spiritual, solid enough to embrace but refined enough to perceive realities your earthly senses could never detect. You are recognizably yourself. Your face, your essence, your being—all intact but improved, clarified, beautified, freed from the limitations matter imposed.

And the first thing you see is her face.

Your guardian, whom you never saw on Earth, will be the first being you see in resurrection. She will be there, radiant and joyful, welcoming you to continued life. The relationship that existed invisibly for decades becomes visible in an instant. You will know her. And you will understand, in a flood of recognition, how thoroughly you were accompanied through every step of your mortal journey.

This process has been accomplished countless times. It is refined, reliable, tested across billions of resurrections on millions of worlds. Angels don't experiment with mortal survival. They execute a procedure that works, every time, without fail, for every soul deemed worthy of continued existence.

Death, then, is not something to fear. It's something to understand. Your guardian knows the process, the route, the destination. When the time comes—whether tomorrow or decades from now—she will be ready. And when you open your eyes on the other side, you will discover that everything you read about angels, everything you learned about their ministry, everything you hoped might be true—it was all real. And she was there all along, faithful beyond measure, waiting for the moment you would finally see her face.

## The Journey Together

Your relationship with your guardian doesn't end at resurrection. It deepens.

On the mansion worlds, you'll finally meet face to face. You'll see her as she truly is—a being of light and intelligence, radiant with purpose and sincerity. You'll learn her name. You'll hear about all the times she intervened on your behalf, the dangers she steered you away from, the opportunities she arranged. You'll understand how thoroughly you were loved and how expertly you were guided.

And then you'll continue forward together. Your guardian accompanies you through the mansion worlds, through the constellation training spheres, through much of the local universe career. She doesn't leave you until you've developed far enough to no longer need her.

Many guardian seraphim have escorted their mortal charges for thousands of years. The bond that forms is one of the most profound relationships in all creation.

## Hidden By Design

Your guardian has been with you for decades. She's watched you at your best and your worst. She's coordinated circumstances, strengthened conscience, recorded choices. Yet you've never consciously perceived her. Why?

The simple answer: because you're not ready. Not as judgment—as fact. Your consciousness is tuned to material frequencies. You perceive what your physical senses detect: light, sound, touch, taste, smell. Your guardian operates at frequencies beyond material detection. It's not that she's hiding. It's that you lack the equipment to perceive her.

But there's more to it than sensory limitation. Even if you could be given the ability to see her, it might hinder your development. Right now, every moral choice you make is *yours*. You own it completely. You can't attribute your courage to her presence or blame your failures on her absence. You're developing authentic character—not performing for an audience.

If she were visible, that would change. You'd make choices to please her. You'd seek her approval. You'd rely on her guidance instead of strengthening your own judgment. Her invisibility protects your authenticity.

One day—after death, after resurrection—you'll see her face. And in that moment, you'll understand: she was there the whole time. Every struggle you thought you faced alone, you faced with her. Every victory you credited entirely to yourself involved her coordination. Every time you chose right despite temptation, she was strengthening the voice of conscience.

You didn't see her because you didn't need to. You needed to become yourself first. And she was patient enough to wait.

## THE DESTINY GUARDIANS

Some guardians receive a special designation: destiny guardians. These are seraphim assigned to mortals who have achieved specific cosmic significance—people whose decisions and actions will influence large numbers of others, who hold positions of unusual trust or responsibility, or who have demonstrated exceptional spiritual attainment.

You may or may not have a destiny guardian. That's not a judgment of your worth but a recognition of your role in the divine plan. Every mortal matters profoundly. But some mortals occupy positions where their choices ripple out to affect thousands or millions of others. These individuals receive enhanced angelic attention.

Even if you don't have a destiny guardian, you have *a* guardian. And that guardian considers you her primary mission, her sacred trust, the soul she has covenanted to deliver safely to eternity if you're willing to make that journey.

## Walking Accompanied

Knowing that your guardian exists changes nothing about your freedom or your responsibility. You still make your own choices. You still face your own consequences. You still develop your own character through your own efforts. But it should change your sense of support.

You are not fighting alone. You are not navigating life without help. When you feel most isolated, you are observed and accompanied. When you face decisions that terrify you, someone who knows you completely is working to arrange the best possible outcome. When you fall, a loving presence helps you rise. When you succeed, a joyful companion celebrates with you.

Your guardian angel is not a good luck charm or a cosmic butler. She is a minister of mercy, a coordinator of opportunity, a recorder of your authentic self, and the deliverer of your soul to your next destination.

She is real. She is yours. She is already at work.

And one day you'll meet her. You'll look into the face of the being who has known you longer and better than anyone except God himself. And you'll understand just how deeply you have been loved, how expertly you have been guided, and how thoroughly you have never, ever been alone.

But your guardian hasn't worked alone. She's had help—faithful partners who've served alongside her every step of the way.

11

# CHERUBIM AND SANOBIM

IF SERAPHIM ARE THE PRIMARY MINISTERING SPIRITS OF THE LOCAL universe, cherubim and sanobim are their essential partners. These beings work alongside seraphim in nearly every assignment, providing complementary abilities and perspectives. They are younger, less experienced, and more limited in capability than seraphim, but they are absolutely vital to effective angelic operation. This team approach ensures that every assignment receives the full range of capabilities needed for success.

> *Cherubim and sanobim are by nature very near the morontia level of existence, and they prove to be most efficient in the borderland work of the physical, morontial, and spiritual domains.*[1]

## CREATED AS HELPERS

Cherubim and sanobim are created by the Universe Mother Spirit specifically to serve as helpers and associates for seraphim. They come into existence with intelligence and personality but without the full range of abilities their superiors possess. They are designed to complement, not duplicate.

As do their superiors, these lesser angels must be trained.

> *When assigned to a planet, cherubim enter the local courses of train-ing, including a study of planetary usages and languages. The minis-tering spirits of time are all bilingual, speaking the language of the local universe of their origin and that of their native superuniverse. By study in the schools of the realms they acquire additional tongues.*[2]

The cherubim assigned to work alongside your guardian angel speaks your language, understands your culture, and has studied Earth's history and social structures. They don't arrive randomly assigned; they arrive as trained specialists.

And their education never stops.

> *Cherubim and sanobim, like seraphim and all other orders of spirit beings, are continuously engaged in efforts at self improvement. Only such as the subordinate beings of power control and energy direction are incapable of progression; all creatures having actual or potential personality volition seek new achievements.*[3]

This dedication to continuous learning means your guardian's cherubim associate is constantly growing in capability, wisdom, and effectiveness. They take their supporting role seriously—and they're always working to do it better.

Each cherubim pairs with a seraphim in a working partnership that often lasts for thousands of years. This partnership is not hierarchical in the sense of master and servant. It's collaborative. The seraphim leads, but the cherubim contributes essential capabilities that make the partnership effective.

## The Seraphim-Cherubim Partnership

When receiving an assignment as guardian, she doesn't work alone. Every seraphim partners with a cherubim associate and is assisted by sanobim helpers who will serve as her complements throughout that assignment.

> *Cherubim and sanobim are inherently associated, functionally united. One is an energy positive personality; the other, energy negative. The right-hand deflector, or positively charged angel, is the cherubim—the senior or controlling personality. The left-hand deflector, or negatively charged angel, is the sanobim—the complement of being. Each type of angel is very limited in solitary function; hence they usually serve in pairs.*[4]

This cherubim becomes intimately involved in the guardian ministry. She observes the same mortal, participates in the same planning, shares in the same victories and disappointments.

> *In all essential endowments cherubim and sanobim are similar to seraphim. They have the same origin but not always the same destiny. They are wonderfully intelligent, marvelously efficient, touchingly affectionate, and almost human. They are the lowest order of angels, hence all the nearer of kin to the more progressive types of human beings on the evolutionary worlds.*[5]

The cherubim brings a different perspective. Where the seraphim might focus on long-term spiritual development, the cherubim might notice immediate practical needs. Where the seraphim coordinates with higher authorities, the cherubim manages details and handles communications. Where the seraphim makes major decisions, the cherubim ensures those decisions are implemented effectively.

This partnership makes both beings more effective than either could be alone. The seraphim gains from the cherubim's different viewpoint and specialized capabilities. The cherubim learns from the seraphim's greater experience and broader perspective. Together, they provide better care than either could provide independently.

## Evolutionary Potential

Here's what makes cherubim truly remarkable: they can evolve into seraphim.

Cherubim are not permanently limited to their helper status. After extensive experience and achievement, a cherubim can undergo transformation and become a seraphim in her own right. This is not automatic or guaranteed. It requires sustained excellence, growth in capability, and often thousands of years of faithful duty. But it's possible.

When a cherubim achieves this status, she gains the full range of seraphic abilities and can be assigned to any seraphic role. She is no longer a helper; she is a primary minister in her own right. And she often brings to her new status insights and capabilities developed through her long experience as a cherubim.

This evolutionary potential means that cherubim are not second-class beings. They are in development, beings with genuine potential for advancement, helpers who may one day become leaders. This gives cherubim work dignity and purpose beyond just assisting others. They are building their own future while serving in their current role.

Many of the Mansion World Teachers—angels who educate newly resurrected mortals on the first several mansion worlds—are former cherubim who achieved seraphic status and then chose to specialize in teaching. Their experience as helpers makes them particularly effective educators. They understand what it's like to serve, to learn, to grow through patient effort. And they bring that understanding to their teaching.

Think of them as support staff. This is not a solo operation. Your guardian is part of a vast, intricate network of celestial beings all working toward the same goal: helping you choose eternal life.

12

# MIDWAYERS

## EARTH'S PERMANENT CITIZENS

Midwayers are unlike any other beings in creation. They are not angels—they don't travel between worlds. They are not mortals—they don't die and resurrect. They are permanent planetary citizens, beings who live on Earth from age to age, watching civilizations rise and fall, working quietly to uplift humanity, and serving as an invisible bridge between the material and spiritual realms.

There are thousands of midwayers on Earth. They have been here for hundreds of thousands of years. They will remain here long after every human currently alive has died and moved on. They are Earth's invisible helpers.

## Type and Origin

Midwayers exist in two distinct groups with very different origins.

Primary midwayers are the older group. They were produced hundreds of thousands of years ago through a unique process involving the corporeal staff of the Planetary Prince—superhuman beings who came to Earth to help guide early human development.

Primary midwayers are more spiritual than material. They can manipulate matter in limited ways. They operate in dimensions slightly removed from purely physical reality. They are intelligent, cultured, and devoted to the welfare of humanity.

Secondary midwayers came into existence much later, descended from the offspring of Adam and Eve—the Material Son and Daughter who came to Earth as biological uplifters (explained in another book). Through a similar but distinct process, their descendants produced the secondary midwayers. These beings are more material than the primary midwayers, though still operating between the physical and spiritual realms.

The two orders worked separately for many ages. But eventually they united under common leadership and now function as a single corps dedicated to planetary assistance.

These two orders of midwayers are not random mutations. They are not cosmic flukes or unintended byproducts of celestial administration. They were designed, planned, and brought into existence for specific purposes.

> *Neither of these groups is an evolutionary accident; both are essential features in the predetermined plans of the universe architects.*[1]

Their existence on Earth was planned long before they came into being. They serve purposes designed into the tapestry of planetary development.

The two orders bring different capabilities to their shared mission. Primary midwayers, being more spiritual in nature, resemble angels more than they do mortals.

> *They are energized intellectually and spiritually by the angelic technique and are uniform in intellectual status.*[2]

Secondary midwayers, being more material, are much more like human beings.

Each order excels in different domains. Primary midwayers can work
with spiritual energies and coordinate with celestial ministers.
Secondary midwayers excel at physical manipulation and material-
realm operations.

But because they can achieve perfect synchrony with each other,
together they can utilize the entire spectrum of energies—from the
gross physical power of material worlds through transitional energies
to the higher spiritual forces of celestial realms. Working together,
they bridge the gap between matter and spirit.

## MIDWAYER MINISTRY

Midwayers serve as living bridges between the material and spiritual
realms. Because they exist partly in both dimensions, they can facilitate certain types of communication and coordination that purely
spiritual beings cannot accomplish as easily. They work closely with
seraphim, providing the material component of combined spiritual-
material ministry.

But their specific duties depend on whether a planet is normal or
isolated. On most inhabited worlds—planets that haven't experienced
rebellion or default—midwayers follow established patterns of
service.

*On normal worlds the primary midwayers maintain their service as
the intelligence corps and as celestial entertainers in behalf of the
Planetary Prince, while the secondary ministers continue their cooperation with the Adamic regime of furthering the cause of progressive planetary civilization.*[4]

Earth is not a normal world. Our Planetary Prince fell into rebellion.
Our Adam and Eve defaulted on their biological uplift mission. So the

midwayers here took on emergency duties never intended for them. They became custodians, guardians, and emergency administrators— roles they've maintained for nearly 200,000 years.

> *The planetary work of both primary and secondary midwayers is varied and diverse on the numerous individual worlds of a universe, but on the normal and average planets their activities are very different from the duties which occupy their time on isolated spheres, such as Earth.*[5]

One duty remains constant across all worlds, whether normal or isolated. Primary midwayers serve as planetary historians.

> *The primary midwayers are the planetary historians who, from the time of the arrival of the Planetary Prince to the age of settled light and life, formulate the pageants and design the portrayals of planetary history for the exhibits of the planets on the system headquarters worlds.*[6]

They preserve evolutionary knowledge for displays on high. They have witnessed the entire history of human civilization. They remember what has been forgotten, what was lost when libraries burned or civilizations collapsed. They are the keepers of planetary memory, the witnesses who know what really happened across the ages.

## A Unique Position

Midwayers occupy a place in the cosmic order unlike any other beings. Their classification reveals their remarkable versatility and their ultimate destiny.

> *The midway creatures have a threefold classification: They are properly classified with the ascending Sons of God; they are factually grouped with the orders of permanent citizenship, while they are functionally reckoned with the ministering spirits of time because of*

*their intimate and effective association with the angelic hosts in the work of serving mortal man on the individual worlds of space.*[7]

This threefold nature defines everything they are and everything they do. They are permanent citizens of Earth, yet their ultimate destiny is Paradise ascent. They function as ministering spirits alongside angels, yet they are not angels. They serve mortals, yet they are classified among ascending Sons of God.

This unique classification means that midwayers bridge categories no other beings can. They understand mortality because they live among mortals for hundreds of thousands of years. They understand spirit reality because they're energized and encircuited by celestial techniques. They understand time because they experience it across ages. They understand eternity because they never perish.

No other order of beings combines permanent planetary citizenship with eventual Paradise ascension. Angels don't stay permanently on one world. Mortals don't remain visible witnesses across civilizations. Only midwayers occupy this singular position—rooted in one world, serving across ages, yet destined for cosmic destinations far beyond their planet of origin.

## THE GREAT DIVISION

Not all midwayers remained loyal to divine purposes. When Lucifer rebelled (addressed in a separate book)—when the System Sovereign chose to reject divine authority and institute his own administration approximately 200,000 years ago—the consequences reached across the entire local system. Angels fell. Midwayers fell. Countless beings were lost.

The toll among the midwayers of our world was devastating. Of the original 50,000 primary midwayers, 40,119 joined the rebellion—more than 80 percent. Of the 1,984 secondary midwayers, 873 aligned themselves with the rebel cause. These disloyal midwayers, along with rebel seraphim and cherubim, remained active on Earth for ages, operating under the leadership of Caligastia, Earth's deposed Planetary Prince.

The rebellion affected more than just midwayers. Among the angelic orders, the greatest losses occurred in the fourth group—the administrator angels normally assigned to system capitals. Approximately one-third of these seraphim followed their leaders into rebellion. One-third of the planetary angelic helpers assigned to Material Sons were deceived. Even some cherubim and transition ministers were ensnared. The ancient writer who spoke of the dragon's tail sweeping a third part of the stars of heaven and casting them down in darkness was describing a real catastrophe that swept through the celestial administration of this local system.

The rebellion happened. It was devastating. Earth still bears its scars. But the active phase is finished. The war is won.


## The United Midwayers

Today, the midwayers who serve Earth are a unified corps combining the loyal remnant of both orders. They are governed alternately by the senior member of each order and work in perfect cooperation with the seraphic planetary government. Every single midwayer currently active on this planet is of honorable standing, fully loyal, and completely dedicated to helping humanity recover from rebellion and advance toward spiritual enlightenment.

These are not your enemies. They are your invisible friends, your planetary guardians. They work as messengers, sentinels, contact personalities, and progress helpers. They assist the seraphim in countless ways. They serve as liaison associates for the planetary reserve corps of destiny—those humans being prepared for special service during times of planetary crisis or advancement.

Many phenomena traditionally attributed to angels were actually performed by midwayers. When the early teachers of Jesus's gospel were thrown into prison and "an angel of the Lord by night opened the prison doors," it was a midwayer who performed the work. When

Peter was delivered from prison after James was killed, it was a secondary midwayer—not an angel—who accomplished the rescue.

## RESIDENT HELPERS

What makes midwayers so remarkable is their permanence. Angels come and go. Mortals live and die. But midwayers remain, generation after generation, age after age. They remember Earth's entire spiritual history and have witnessed the full scope of human civilization. They understand where humanity has been and where it needs to go.

They are invested in Earth's future in a way no other beings can be. This is their home. Their destiny is bound to this planet's destiny. When Earth finally achieves the advanced spiritual status it's meant to reach—when humanity becomes enlightened and this world enters the stages of light and life—the midwayers will still be here, celebrating the fulfillment of purposes they have served for hundreds of thousands of years.

Humans are not the only intelligent life on this planet. Invisible but real, silent but active, the midwayers work constantly to help humanity survive, grow, and eventually triumph over all the obstacles that rebellion and isolation have placed in the way.

They are Earth's helpers, the permanent residents who will never abandon this troubled sphere, no matter how long it takes for healing and enlightenment to arrive. And they are working on your behalf right now, whether you know it or not, whether you believe in them or not. Because that's what loyal servants do. They serve, patiently and faithfully, until the work is complete.

That kind of loyalty is precious. That kind of love is holy. No mortal will ever know what it means to serve one place, one people, for ages that dwarf recorded history. Imagine what it means to love a planet for hundreds of thousands of years. To watch civilizations rise and fall, to see the same mistakes repeated across millennia, to witness suffering you cannot prevent—and yet to remain hopeful. To continue serving. To keep faith that someday, eventually, this world will be brought to light.

The midwayers are married to this planet. In rebellion and isolation, through darkness and despair, when evil seemed triumphant and hope seemed foolish—they stayed.

These natives know your world in ways you never will. They've witnessed the most inspiring acts of compassion, the forests that have sheltered the most profound prayers, the homes that have held the strongest love. They are the silent witnesses to humanity's true history—not only the wars and kingdoms, but the small victories of the human spirit that make those wars bearable.

Every generation of humans that ever lived has been accompanied by these unseen companions who never stopped believing that light would eventually triumph over darkness. They've seen what you're capable of. They know what you could become. And they're working, quietly and ceaselessly, to help you get there. Because this is their home too, and your victory is theirs.

And right now, while you live your brief mortal life, these ancient beings are watching over this world with a majestic faithfulness. They've outlasted empires. They'll outlast your worries. And when this planet finally reaches the light, when humanity finally becomes what it was created to be, the midwayers will be here to see it.

And then? When Earth finally achieves light and life, when their agelong service is complete, when the work is finished? The loyal midwayers who have served this world so faithfully will receive their reward.

*Midwayers remain for long periods on an inhabited world, but if faithful to their trust, they will eventually and most certainly be recognized for their agelong service in maintaining the sovereignty of the Creator Son; they will be duly rewarded for their patient ministry to the material mortals on their world of time and space.*

*Sooner or later all accredited midway creatures will be mustered into the ranks of the ascending Sons of God and will be duly initiated into the long adventure of the Paradise ascent in company with those very mortals of animal origin, their earth brethren, whom they so jealously guarded and so effectively served during the long planetary sojourn.*[8]

The midwayers who watched over your ancestors, who stood invisible beside you in your darkest moments—these same beings will one day walk beside you on the Paradise journey. The servants will become companions. The guardians will become fellow pilgrims.

Together—mortals and midwayers, humans and the ancient beings who loved us through rebellion's darkness—we will all reach Paradise. Because that's where this journey has always been leading. That's what all this faithful service has been for.

The midwayers know this. They've known it for ages. And they've never stopped working to help you get there.

13

# ORGANIZATION AND VELOCITY

ANGELS ARE NOT FREELANCERS. THEY OPERATE WITHIN SOPHISTICATED organizational structures across worlds, systems, and entire universes. Understanding how angels organize reveals that divine administration is not random or improvised but systematic, efficient, and thoroughly coordinated.

## HIERARCHICAL STRUCTURE

Angels organize into clear hierarchies based on function, experience, and capability. This is not about superiority or inferiority but about appropriate organization—ensuring that every function has clear leadership and that coordination flows smoothly between levels.

Each level has designated leadership. A being of extraordinary capability and experience leads each company. Higher-ranking creatures of light—those with proven excellence in administration and coordination—lead battalions, units, legions, and armies.

Seraphim organize into companies of 144 angels. Twelve companies form a battalion of 1,728 beings. Twelve battalions constitute a unit of 20,736 seraphim. Twelve units form a legion of 248,832 celestial persons. And twelve legions make up an army of approximately 3 million angels.

This organizational structure allows for efficient communication, clear lines of authority, and diverse activities across vast numbers of angels working in diverse locations. When a planet needs additional guardians, the request flows up through these channels. When seraphim need reassignment after completing their charge, the organizational structure facilitates those transitions.

This system ensures that angels working on specific worlds or with specific mortals receive the resources, information, and support they need. The organizational overhead isn't wasted effort—it's essential infrastructure.

## SPEED AND TRAVEL

Angels don't teleport instantly. They travel at specific velocities through space. The midway creatures and certain others can attain double velocity—372,560 miles per second. Seraphim travel at approximately three times the speed of light.

> *Transporters take on energy for flight while in transit and recuperate personal power at the end of the journey. Ascenders must depend upon seraphic transport in advancing from world to world until after the last rest of sleep and the eternal awakening on Paradise.*

> *The fifth group of supervisor seraphim operate as personality transporters, carrying beings to and from the headquarters of the constellations. Such transport seraphim, while in flight from one sphere to another, are fully conscious of their velocity, direction, and astronomic whereabouts.*[1]

> *They are not traversing space as would an inanimate projectile. They may pass near one another during space flight without the least danger of collision. They are fully able to vary speed of progression and to alter direction of flight, even to change destinations if their*

*directors should so instruct them at any space junction of the universe intelligence circuits.*

*These transit personalities are so organized that they can simultaneously utilize all three of the universally distributed lines of energy, each having a clear space velocity of 186,280 miles per second.*

*These transporters are thus able to superimpose velocity of energy upon velocity of power until they attain an average speed on their long journeys varying anywhere from 555,000 to almost 559,000 of your miles per second of your time. The velocity is affected by the mass and proximity of neighboring matter and by the strength and direction of the near-by main circuits of universe power.*

*There are numerous types of beings, similar to the seraphim, who are able to traverse space, and who also are able to transport other beings who have been properly prepared.*[2]

## SOLITARY MESSENGERS

These specialized beings, created for rapid communication, travel at speeds far exceeding seraphim. They are capable of crossing universe distances in relatively short periods. When urgent messages must reach remote locations quickly, Solitary Messengers carry them.

*They are the highest type of perfect and confidential personality available in all realms for the quick transmission of important and urgent messages when it is inexpedient to utilize either the broadcast service or the reflectivity mechanism.*

*They serve in an endless variety of assignments, helping out the spiritual and material beings of the realms, particularly where the element of time is involved. Of all orders assigned to the services of the superuniverse domains, they are the highest and most versatile personalized beings who can come so near to defying time and space.*

*Solitary Messengers are, therefore, generally used for dispatch and service in those situations where personality is essential to the achievement of the assignment, and where it is desired to avoid the loss of time which would be occasioned by the sending of any other readily available type of personal messenger. They are the only definitely personalized beings who can synchronize with the combined universal currents of the grand universe.*

*Their velocity in traversing space is variable, depending on a great variety of interfering influences, but the record shows that on the journey to fulfill this mission, the associate messenger proceeded at the rate of 841,621,642,000 of your miles per second of your time.*[3]

These velocities require coordination. Angels and other celestial servants can't simply depart whenever convenient. They must work with transport schedules, plan routes, and allow for travel time. The organizational systems that manage these logistics are complex and sophisticated, ensuring that they arrive where needed when needed despite the limitations of finite velocity.

## Universal Order

Some might imagine that spiritual beings operate spontaneously, guided only by intuition or immediate divine inspiration. The reality is quite different.

The universe contains trillions of inhabited worlds. Countless mortals require ministry at various stages of development. Adequate administrative systems must function efficiently across enormous distances. Complex plans must coordinate the work of billions of beings serving diverse functions.

This requires organization—clear structures, defined roles, efficient communication, reliable coordination. Without such organization, chaos would result.

Angelic organization ensures reliability, that resources reach where they're needed, that nothing essential is neglected, and that divine purposes are executed through carefully designed systems staffed by competent beings working cooperatively.

You benefit from this organization every day. Your guardian receives support from higher administrators. Communication systems keep her connected to sources of information and guidance. Transport systems ensure that sleeping souls reach the resurrection halls. Recording systems preserve everything of value from your life.

The angels working on your behalf are not isolated individuals hoping for the best. They're part of an extensive, expertly coordinated system designed to ensure your survival and facilitate your progression. That should give you tremendous feelings of security and peace.

The universe is not chaotic. It's orderly. And the quality of that order reflects the character of God himself—purposeful, efficient, reliable, and dedicated to the welfare of every ascending soul.

This organization isn't bureaucracy for its own sake. It exists to ensure you don't get lost in the sprawling cosmos. When you die, the system knows where to send you. When you need help, the hierarchy delivers it. This structure guarantees your successful and eternal survival.

# 14

# THE REALITY OF ANGELIC PRESENCE

IF ANGELS ARE REAL AND ACTIVELY MINISTERING TO MORTALS, WHY don't people see them? Why is their presence not obvious? Why does so much of human experience feel devoid of supernatural assistance?

These are fair questions. The answers reveal important truths about how spiritual reality interfaces with material existence and why faith requires some degree of uncertainty.

## BEYOND PERCEPTION

Angels exist at energy frequencies your physical senses cannot detect. Your eyes perceive electromagnetic radiation between roughly 380 and 700 nanometers—the visible light spectrum. Anything outside that range is invisible to you: ultraviolet, infrared, radio waves, X-rays. These frequencies are real. They're constantly present. You simply lack the biological equipment to perceive them.

Angels operate at frequencies beyond material perception entirely. They exist in dimensions that interpenetrate material reality but remain undetectable by material instruments. This isn't mystical—it's mechanical. Your retinas aren't designed to detect spiritual phenomena any more than they're designed to detect radio waves. The limitation is yours, not theirs.

Think of it as a spectrum issue. You're currently equipped to perceive only the material frequency. After resurrection, you'll have higher senses capable of perceiving higher realities. But right now it's like someone trying to see radio waves with their naked eyes. The limitation isn't malicious. It's simply how frequencies work.

## Hidden Benefits

Angelic invisibility isn't accidental. It's designed. Even if you could be given the ability to see angels—eyes modified to perceive certain frequencies, senses expanded beyond material limitation—it wouldn't be wise. Not yet. Not at this stage of your development. Because invisible help protects your becoming and your spiritual integrity.

Consider what would happen if angels were visible:

**Faith would become unnecessary.** Right now, when you choose to trust divine goodness despite suffering, when you persist in seeking truth despite discouragement, when you act with integrity despite no visible reward—you're developing faith. Real faith. The kind that transforms consciousness and builds eternal character.

But if angels were obvious? Faith collapses into certainty. And certainty doesn't develop anything. You'd know goodness wins because you can *see* the armies of angels. You'd trust God because the proof is standing next to you. That's not faith—that's calculation. Faith requires risk. Invisibility creates the space for that risk.

**Free will would become compromised.** Right now, your choices are authentically yours. When you choose courage, you *own* that courage. When you show mercy, it emerges from your genuine character—not performance for an audience.

But if your guardian were visible? She becomes the audience. You start making choices to please her, to earn her approval, to avoid her disappointment. You'd be playing to the judge instead of becoming yourself.

Children with hovering parents never develop full autonomy. They're always performing, always seeking approval, never learning to trust their own judgment. Invisibility protects your agency. You remain the author of your story.

**Spiritual growth would become short-circuited.** The hardest spiritual lessons come from wrestling with uncertainty. Why does God allow suffering? Why isn't goodness rewarded immediately? Why does evil sometimes seem to triumph? Why do prayers go unanswered?

These questions torture people. They also transform them. The person who maintains integrity through doubt develops stronger character than the person who never doubts because proof is obvious. The soul that chooses love despite suffering understands love more deeply than the soul that loves because love always yields pleasant results.

If angels were visible, these questions would have easy answers. And easy answers produce shallow souls.

God could make angels visible. The technology exists—celestial beings can materialize, energy can be manipulated, human senses could be enhanced. It's not a limitation of divine power. It's a choice. A design choice.

Angels work in the dark because humans grow in the dark. Not the darkness of evil—the darkness of uncertainty, where faith ignites, where character forms, where real choice becomes possible.

One day, after resurrection, you'll see clearly. Angels will be visible. Proof will be obvious. God will be unmistakable. But by then, you'll have already become someone. Someone shaped by choices made without proof. Someone forged in uncertainty. Someone who chose truth when truth was hidden, who trusted goodness when goodness seemed absent, who persisted in integrity when integrity offered no visible reward.

And that someone—the person you became in the dark—is the person angels were protecting by remaining invisible. The invisibility isn't a bug. It's the feature that makes your development possible.

## When They Do Appear

Throughout history, angels have occasionally materialized and appeared to human beings in visible form. These appearances are rare, but they are real. How is this possible if angels exist in dimensions above material reality?

The answer lies in sophisticated energy manipulation involving multiple orders of celestial beings working in coordination. Certain specialized beings—physical-energy manipulators and power directors—possess the ability to control and modify energy currents. When angels need to become visible, these energy specialists create the necessary conditions for spirit beings to manifest in forms perceptible to mortal senses.

This is not simple work. It requires precise coordination between beings who can manipulate physical reality, those who work with mental energies, and those who handle spiritual forces. The compound manipulators, in particular, specialize in associating these three types of energy—physical, mental, and spiritual—making it possible for purely spiritual beings to temporarily assume visible material form.

Such appearances serve specific purposes. Angels don't materialize for entertainment or to prove their existence. They appear when necessary—to deliver crucial messages, to prevent disaster, to mark moments of extraordinary spiritual significance. The effort and coordination required ensure that materializations occur only when truly warranted.

Most humans will never see an angel in this life. But that doesn't mean angelic appearances don't happen. They do. Just rarely. And always for good reason.

## Limits of Angelic Intervention

If angels are real and constantly present, why do people suffer? Why do children die of cancer? Why does genocide happen? Why do natural disasters destroy innocent lives? If your guardian watches over you, why didn't she prevent that accident, that illness, that loss?

These are not theoretical questions. They're visceral, personal, and potentially deal-breaking. If angels exist but stand by while horror unfolds, what good are they?

The answer requires honesty about angelic limits, about Earth's unique disadvantages, and about the nature of evolutionary existence. It won't satisfy completely—nothing could. But it offers a framework for understanding why protection is partial and suffering persists.

When humans choose cruelty, violence, or negligence, angels cannot force them to choose differently. This means true evil—abuse, murder, brutality—continues because free will is untouchable. Angels will not prevent atrocities by controlling minds. Real personhood requires real choice, which means real consequences, including horrific ones.

Your guardian watches you make destructive decisions and cannot stop you. She grieves your choices but respects your agency absolutely.

Angels work within physical systems and laws, not outside them. They cannot cure all diseases, prevent all accidents, or suspend gravity to save you from falling. They can sometimes minimize danger, arrange fortuitous timing, coordinate help—but they cannot make the material world operate contrary to its designed patterns.

This means natural devastation—disease, earthquakes, genetic disorders, random accidents—continues because matter follows laws.

Angels don't author these tragedies, but they can't prevent them either.

Some suffering has no moral cause, no free will component. It's simply the consequence of living in an evolutionary, imperfect, material world that hasn't yet achieved the perfection it's moving toward.

Earth has some unique disadvantages. Suffering here is worse than on normal worlds. This planet experienced rebellion—Lucifer's rejection of divine authority and Caligastia's betrayal as Planetary Prince. Earth was quarantined, cut off from normal celestial circuits and assistance. Guided human evolution ceased. For millennia, this world has operated in spiritual isolation, deprived of the full ministry and aid that other planets receive.

The effects linger. Social systems remain primitive. Violence persists. Suffering multiplies. This is not how inhabited worlds are supposed to develop. Earth is a casualty of rebellion, and angels work within the wreckage left behind. Your guardian does her best in circumstances she didn't create and cannot fully repair. She works with limitations imposed by rebellion, isolation, and planetary immaturity. If you're angry about suffering, direct that anger toward those who betrayed this world, not toward those trying to salvage it.

Angels cannot shield you from all difficulty. Even if they could eliminate all suffering, they wouldn't. Challenge is essential to growth. A life without difficulty produces weak, undeveloped character. Strength comes from struggle. Courage develops through facing fear. Compassion grows from experiencing pain.

Angels understand this. They don't rescue you from every hardship but help you grow through appropriate challenges. But—and this is critical—not every instance of suffering serves growth. Cancer that kills a child isn't a divine lesson. Genocide isn't character development. Natural disasters aren't cosmic classrooms. Some suffering is simply the cost of evolutionary existence, the result of random material processes operating without moral intent.

Angels don't orchestrate tragedies for your benefit. They work within tragedies you experience despite their efforts to minimize harm.

When you suffer, your guardian suffers with you. She's not indifferent, not detached, not calmly observing your pain as "necessary for growth." She grieves when you grieve. She experiences frustration at her limits. She wishes she could do more.

Material existence is harsh. Evolutionary worlds are flawed. Free will produces tragedy. Natural law operates without regard for individual well-being.

But this isn't the whole story. Suffering on Earth doesn't exhaust divine response. Victims of trauma receive special ministry in resurrection. Justice denied here finds satisfaction there. Healing begins in this life but continues far beyond it.

The universe bends toward mercy, even when Earth doesn't. That doesn't erase present pain or justify past horror. But it offers hope that suffering, though real and terrible, is not the final word.

Angels can't prevent all suffering, but they refuse to abandon you *in* suffering. That's not comfort enough when grief is fresh. But it's something. It's faithfulness when omnipotence is absent.

Your guardian has watched you suffer, worked within intolerable limits, and stayed faithful anyway. Because she knows what you'll eventually know: that the journey from here to hereafter, though difficult, leads to destinations where suffering no longer exists and every tear is wiped away.

That day will come. But until it does, angels work within the mess—limited but faithful, and hoping you'll understand that their inability to prevent all pain doesn't mean they don't care. It means they're working within a system they didn't create, doing everything they're permitted to do, and refusing to abandon you even when they can't rescue you.

# Recognizing Angelic Ministry

Even though you can't see angels, you can recognize their influence if you know what to watch for:

**Inexplicable rescues.** When you escape danger by margins too narrow to be mere luck, when things align to protect you against odds that don't make sense, your guardian may have intervened. Not always—sometimes luck is just luck—but patterns of improbable rescue suggest invisible assistance.

**Coordinated human help.** When you meet exactly the right person at exactly the right moment, when opportunities appear or friends call just when you need them—these may be angelic coordination. Midwayers and seraphim working together can arrange such events.

**Strengthened intuition.** When you suddenly know something you have no logical way of knowing, when clear thoughts emerge in moments of crisis, when you feel strong impulses toward certain choices—your guardian may be influencing your consciousness.

**Unexplained comfort.** When grief lifts unexpectedly, when peace descends in the midst of chaos, when you feel accompanied though physically alone—angels often produces such effects. They can influence emotional states, providing comfort and courage when needed.

**Patterns of growth.** When you look back and see that challenges arranged themselves in sequences that forced your development, when difficulties arrived in doses you could barely handle but did handle, when your life reveals a curriculum you didn't consciously design—angels may have been coordinating your edification.

These examples are not proof. They're hints, suggestions, patterns that point toward invisible assistance.

Understanding what angels cannot do is important. But understanding what they *can* do is equally vital. These loving ministers:

**Stay with you through every moment.** You are never alone in your pain, even when it feels that way.

**Preserve identity perfectly.** When suffering ends in death, she captures everything essential about you for resurrection. Nothing is lost.

**Prepare reunion with the departed.** The ones you've lost are waiting for the day you'll see them again.

Faith still requires trust beyond certainty. But thoughtful observation reveals fingerprints of ministry that comfort and encourage those willing to see.

15

# YOUR JOURNEY WITH ANGELS



Your relationship with angels is not temporary. It doesn't end at death or even at resurrection. They accompany you through stages of existence so vast that mortal imagination can barely comprehend them. Understanding this journey reveals the full scope of the profound partnership between ascending mortals and ministering spirits.

## FROM BIRTH TO CHOICE

You are born without a guardian. Infants don't make moral choices yet, and guardian angels are assigned only when mortals become capable of choosing between right and wrong.

But you're not unprotected during childhood. Group guardians oversee children collectively, watching over their welfare and protecting them within the limits of natural law. These celestials ensure that the population of children receives appropriate spiritual oversight.

Then comes the moment—usually somewhere between ages five and six—when you make your first genuine moral decision. Not just a choice between alternatives, but a recognition of right and wrong with the freedom to choose either. In that moment, something profound changes.

If you choose rightly, if you demonstrate even minimal spiritual receptivity, a seraphim may step forward and claim you. From that point on, you have a guardian.

This guardian knows your choice even if you don't consciously remember it. She sees your potential. And she commits to helping you develop that potential.

As you grow spiritually, you may be promoted from group guardianship to personal guardianship. This means one seraphim focuses exclusively on you, dedicating her full attention to your development. This is not a reward for good behavior but a recognition of your increasing survival potential—an investment of resources where they'll produce the greatest return. Your guardian continues this until death interrupts mortal existence.

## Through Mortal Life

The previous chapters described what your guardian does during your earthly existence—the guidance, the protection, the constant adjustment of circumstances to maximize your spiritual growth. She works within the limits of your free will, never forcing but always facilitating.

What deserves emphasis here is the cumulative nature of this partnership. Over decades, your guardian learns everything about you: your strengths, your weaknesses, the specific temptations that threaten you, the particular encouragements that uplift you. She becomes the universe's foremost expert on your soul.

By the time death approaches, she knows you better than you know yourself. And that knowledge proves essential for what comes next.

## At Death and Resurrection

Death is not the end of the partnership but a critical moment when it becomes absolutely essential.

Your guardian captures your identity pattern as you die. She preserves the record of who you are—personality, memories, relationships, achievements. You are then transported to the mansion world where you'll awaken. This is literal transportation across space, carrying your soul and identity pattern to resurrection halls designed specifically for reassembling ascending mortals.

When the archangel gives the signal, your guardian delivers your identity pattern to those entrusted with constructing your new body. She coordinates with the return of your indwelling spirit. She participates in the profound process required to bring you back into conscious existence.

And she's there when you open your eyes. The first being you see in your new life is the one who safeguarded you through death—your guardian, greeting you by name, welcoming you home.

## On the Mansion Worlds

Your celestial companion doesn't leave you after resurrection. She accompanies you through the seven mansion worlds as you adjust to semi-spirit existence and begin formal training.

She answers questions about your new reality. She helps you understand your new body and its capabilities. She facilitates reunions with loved ones who preceded you in death. She introduces you to the vast array of beings who will contribute to your education.

As you traverse the mansion worlds, her role evolves. Early on, she provides extensive guidance because everything is unfamiliar. Later, as you gain competence and confidence, she steps back, allowing you to exercise greater independence while remaining available for consultation and encouragement.

By the time you complete the seventh mansion world, you've developed significant capability. You understand higher reality. You've mastered basic cosmic concepts. You're ready to graduate to the constellation training spheres.

## Through the Universe

Your guardian continues accompanying you through much of your universe career. She's there when you achieve God fusion—the permanent union of your soul with your indwelling divine fragment, making you truly immortal. She celebrates this milestone with profound joy because it represents the certain success of her long ministry. You will not fail. You will reach Paradise.

She participates in your ongoing education on the constellation worlds and beyond. She watches you develop cosmic consciousness, understanding patterns and purposes that span vast scales. She shares in your discoveries and your growth.

Eventually, you reach a stage where you no longer need her. You've developed sufficient spiritual maturity to continue independently. At this point, your guardian receives new assignments. Her work with you is complete.

But the relationship doesn't simply end. You know each other deeply. You've shared death and resurrection, victories and challenges across ages of development. That bond remains real even as you part ways.

## The Guardian's Ascension

Guardian seraphim are not stationary beings. They themselves can ascend to Paradise.

After completing assignments to multiple mortal charges, after demonstrating excellence in ministry, a guardian may be released from assignment to begin her own Paradise journey. She'll traverse the local universe, the superuniverse, Havona, and eventually reach

Paradise itself—the same journey you're making, though her path differs in specific details.

This means that eventually, far in the future, you might encounter your guardian again. Not as ward and protector but as fellow Paradise citizens. You'll recognize each other. You'll remember the shared journey. You'll celebrate the fact that both of you—the mortal who started as an animal on a primitive world and the angel who served faithfully across ages—have reached the same destination.

That reunion will be sweet beyond measure. Two beings who began so differently, who served each other in such asymmetric ways, will stand together as equals in the presence of God, their individual journeys complete, their partnership remembered with gratitude.

## Angels and Finaliters

When you finally reach Paradise, when you've completed the entire ascension journey and are inducted into the Corps of Mortal Finaliters, you'll receive assignments hither and yon across a vast creation, to serve as perfected beings of divine completion.

And who serves with finaliters? Angels. Specifically, finaliters work alongside ascended seraphim who have completed their own progression. They don't serve finaliters the way guardians serve mortals. They work as colleagues, contributing specialized capabilities to missions that require cooperation between different orders of perfected beings.

Your relationship with angels thus continues even beyond Paradise. Not as helper and helped but as fellow servants working together in God's eternal plans. The partnership that began when a seraphim claimed you as a child continues across eternity, constantly evolving but never entirely ending.

## The Ultimate Destiny

What is the final destiny of angels? The same as yours—eternal service in an ever-expanding universe.

Angels don't retire. They don't reach a point where work ends and eternal leisure begins. Service is their nature, their joy, their purpose. And the universe will always require intelligent, capable, devoted beings willing to minister, facilitate, love and serve.

Your destiny is the same. You'll reach perfection, but perfection doesn't mean stasis. It means readiness for ever-greater work, ever-expanding responsibility, ever-deeper participation in divine purposes.

You and angels share this destiny. Different origins, different capabilities, different paths—but the same ultimate purpose: serving God and his creation across ages without end.


## Perspective

Knowing this journey—understanding that these personalities have ministered to you from childhood and will continue to through death, across countless worlds, and will be your comrades even beyond Paradise—should fundamentally shape how you live now.

**You're not alone.** You never have been. A being of extraordinary capability has invested herself in your welfare. She knows you completely and works tirelessly on your behalf.

**Your life matters.** God doesn't assign angels to worthless projects. The fact that one ministers to you proves your value. You're worth the investment.

**Death is not the end.** Your guardian has already made preparations for your resurrection. She's ready to transport you, to reassemble you, to welcome you. Death is a transition she'll help you navigate successfully.

**The future is limitless.** What awaits you isn't mere survival but adventure—education, growth, relationships, and discoveries that will span ages. Angels will be part of that journey, working alongside you as you progress.

**You're part of something larger.** The universe isn't haphazard. It's purposefully administered by competent beings working cooperatively. You fit into that purpose. Angels facilitate your fit.

Live knowing these truths. You're surrounded by invisible helpers. Your journey extends beyond imagination. And beings of light and love work constantly to ensure you survive, grow, and eventually stand in Paradise as a perfected spirit—the animal-origin human who became divine through choice, effort, and the expert ministry of angels who never gave up on you.

That's the truth about angels.

# EPILOGUE

## A NEW UNDERSTANDING

You began this book with images of wings and halos, harps and clouds, vague spiritual presences offering generic comfort. You end it with something completely different: a detailed, specific, structured picture of actual beings performing real functions in a vast cosmic administration.

Angels are not what you thought they were. They're much better.

They're not identical, interchangeable spirits floating aimlessly through eternity. They're individuals—billions of unique personalities, each with specific capabilities, assignments, and purposes. They work in teams across interstellar distances. They report through clear chains of authority. They perform specialized functions that require expertise and training.

They're not vaguely benevolent. They're specifically helpful. Your guardian knows your name, your history, your potential. She doesn't offer generic blessings, she strengthens specific impulses.

They're not occasional visitors. They're constant companions. From your first moral choice until long after you've reached Paradise, angels work on your behalf. They're there at death, preserving your identity. They're there at resurrection, welcoming you to new life. They're there through the mansion worlds, facilitating your education. They're there as you proceed through the universe, celebrating your victories and supporting you through challenges.

And they're not alone. You've discovered an entire cosmos full of ministering spirits—supernaphim on Paradise, seconaphim in the superuniverses, seraphim in local universes, archangels coordinating resurrections, midwayers serving as permanent planetary helpers. Each order contributes specialized capabilities. Together they form a complete system of ministry that ensures no ascending soul lacks the help needed to live and grow forever.

This is not speculation. This is not religious poetry dressed up as fact. This is the actual structure of angelic reality as revealed in *The Urantia Book*—detailed, specific, and astonishing.

## WHAT THIS MEANS FOR YOU

Understanding the truth about angels should fundamentally change how you experience life.

**You're not isolated.** You live in an ocean of invisible support. Multiple orders of beings work constantly on your behalf. Your guardian watches over you personally. Planetary helpers influence your society. Higher administrators ensure the systems serving you function properly.

**You're not forgotten.** Divine care doesn't stop at creation. God assigns angels—competent, experienced, devoted beings—to ensure that every decent soul receives expert assistance. You matter enough to warrant this investment.

**Death is not the end.** Your guardian has already prepared for your resurrection. She knows exactly what to do when you die. She'll preserve your identity, transport you to your new home, and greet you when you awaken. This is standard procedure, executed countless times, proven reliable.

**Your destiny is big.** What awaits you isn't mere survival but adventure—mansion worlds, constellation spheres, superuniverse training, Havona circuits, Paradise itself, and then eternal life in ever-expanding realms. Angels will accompany you through much of this journey, their work evolving but never ending.

**The universe makes sense.** It's run by competent beings working cooperatively. Angels are the civil service of the cosmos—the skilled workers who make divine administration function smoothly. Knowing they exist should give you tremendous confidence that purposes will be accomplished, promises will be kept, and care will be provided.

## Living With Angels

How should you live, knowing what you now know?

**Not with paranoia.** You don't need to scrutinize every event wondering if angels caused it. You don't need to constantly thank invisible helpers for every good thing. Live normally. Make decisions based on available information. Act as if you're responsible for your own life—because you are.

Angels help, but they don't do your work for you. You must still make good choices, develop your own character, and build your own soul through your own decisions. Angels facilitate; they don't replace personal effort.

Live differently than before:

**Live with confidence.** When genuine difficulty comes, when you need help beyond your own capability, invisible support is available. These beings are watching and will assist if help is appropriate. You can face challenges knowing you're not alone in them.

**Live with gratitude.** Even though you can't see your guardian, you can thank her. Acknowledge her decades of thankless support. Appreciate the system of care that surrounds you. Recognize that what you've called luck might be collaboration, that good fortune might be invisible intervention.

**Live with trust when things go wrong.** When help doesn't arrive, when you face suffering despite angelic presence, trust that limitation serves a purpose. Angels haven't abandoned you. They're helping in ways you can't perceive, or they're allowing (perhaps even coordinating) challenges that will ultimately strengthen you.

Angels cannot prevent all suffering. But they can ensure suffering is never meaningless.

**Live with anticipation.** One day you'll meet your guardian face to face. You'll learn about all the dangers she steered you from, all the opportunities she arranged, all the times she intervened when you thought you were alone. You'll understand just how thoroughly you were accompanied through a journey you thought you walked alone.

That reunion will be sweet beyond measure.

**Live with wonder.** The universe is far more populated, far more organized, and far more purposeful than you imagined. Angels are real. They're here. They're working right now. And their existence proves that reality extends far beyond material perception into dimensions of beauty, order, and purpose that your current senses cannot detect.

Though you can't see them yet, their reality is no less certain than the air you breathe but cannot see.

**Live with wisdom about others.** You may discover that not everyone in your life is ready to hear what you've learned. Some will think you're deluded. Some will dismiss this as fantasy. Some will feel threatened by cosmology that contradicts what they were taught.

This is normal. And it can feel lonely.

You cannot force revelation on anyone. You can only live what you know and let your life demonstrate whether this knowledge produces good fruit. If understanding angels makes you more compassionate, more courageous, more grateful, more alive—people will notice. And some will ask what changed. Then you can tell them.

**Until that day when you see your guardian's face, when you walk those heavenly realms, when invisible reality becomes visible—live in faith.**

Angels are real. They're here. You are surrounded by invisible helpers —expert, devoted, tireless in their care. The universe is teeming with beings who facilitate your eternal life and celebrate your growth.

**You have never walked alone.**

**And now you know it.**

# FROM THE AUTHOR

Thank you for reading. This book is the culmination of twenty years of spiritual seeking, study, and reflection.

If you're willing to share your thoughts, reader reviews make a meaningful difference for independent authors. Thank you so much.

# APPENDIX

## SOURCE REFERENCES

The information in this book is drawn from *The Urantia Book*, a 2,097 page book first published in 1955 that claims to be a revelation presented by celestial beings to clarify and expand human understanding of cosmic reality and our place within it. This book about angels exclusively cites the 1955 edition which is in the public domain.

You may have never heard of it. Or you may have heard of it and dismissed it. That's fine. What matters is whether the information resonates as true, whether it elevates your understanding, whether it helps you live with greater purpose and confidence.

*The Urantia Book* has its critics and its devoted students. It's been called everything from the most important spiritual text of the modern era to elaborate fiction. I'm not asking you to accept it blindly. I'm asking you to read it and *then* decide if you think it is true. I do, and I have read it countless times.

The source is less important than the truth it contains. And if you want to explore further, *The Urantia Book* is available online and in print.

## ABOUT THE SOURCE MATERIAL

*The Urantia Book* is a comprehensive revelatory tome covering a wide variety of subjects including cosmology, philosophy, history and spirituality. It describes the nature of reality from the perspective of celestial beings and provides detailed information about the structure of the universe, the nature of God, the purpose of human existence, and the journey of the soul after death.

The book is organized into 196 papers grouped into four parts:

Part I: The Central and Superuniverses

Part II: The Local Universe

Part III: The History of Urantia (Earth)

Part IV: The Life and Teachings of Jesus

This book, *The Angelic Orders*, draws primarily from Parts I and II, which describe the celestial hierarchies and the structure of creation.

While I do, at times, exercise creative license, my intention is never to stray from what the book discloses as revelatory fact. Any mistakes are mine to own and correct.

*Italicized passages throughout this book are drawn from The Urantia Book, either verbatim or closely paraphrased. Many have been slightly condensed, combined, edited, or adapted for brevity and narrative continuity while preserving the essential meaning and terminology of the original text.*

The following references are organized by chapter to help readers locate the source material corresponding to specific content in this book.

# NOTES

## INTRODUCTION

1. Paper 38, Section 2: Ministering Spirits of the Local Universe, Angelic Natures

## 1. THE ORIGIN OF ANGELS

1. Paper 38, Section 2: Ministering Spirits of the Local Universe, The Seraphim
2. Paper 38, Section 1: Ministering Spirits of the Local Universe, Origin of Seraphim

## 2. SUPERNAPHIM

1. Paper 26, Section 0: Ministering Spirits of the Central Universe, Introduction
2. Paper 27, Section 7: Ministry of the Primary Supernaphim, Conductors of Worship
3. Paper 27, Section 6: Ministry of the Primary Supernaphim, Masters of Philosophy
4. Paper 27, Section 5: Ministry of the Primary Supernaphim, Custodians of Knowledge
5. Paper 27, Section 4: Ministry of the Primary Supernaphim, Directors of Conduct
6. Paper 27, Section 3: Ministry of the Primary Supernaphim, Interpreters of Ethics
7. Paper 27, Section 2: Ministry of the Primary Supernaphim, Chiefs of Assignment
8. Paper 27, Section 1: Ministry of the Primary Supernaphim, Instigators of Rest
9. Paper 26, Section 3: Ministering Spirits of the Central Universe, Pilgrims of Time

## 3. SECONAPHIM

1. Paper 17, Section 3: The Seven Supreme Spirit Groups, The Reflective Spirits
2. Paper 17, Section 3: The Seven Supreme Spirit Groups, The Reflective Spirits
3. Paper 17, Section 3: The Seven Supreme Spirit Groups, The Reflective Spirits
4. Paper 17, Section 3: The Seven Supreme Spirit Groups, The Reflective Spirits
5. Paper 17, Section 3: The Seven Supreme Spirit Groups, The Reflective Spirits
6. Paper 17, Section 3: The Seven Supreme Spirit Groups, The Reflective Spirits
7. Paper 17, Section 3: The Seven Supreme Spirit Groups, The Reflective Spirits
8. Paper 28, Section 4: Ministering Spirits of the Superuniverses, The Primary Seconaphim
9. Paper 28, Section 5, Number 1: Ministering Spirits of the Superuniverses, The Secondary Seconaphim, The Voices of Wisdom
10. Paper 28, Section 5, Number 2: Ministering Spirits of the Superuniverses, The Secondary Seconaphim, The Souls of Philosophy
11. Paper 28, Section 5, Number 3: Ministering Spirits of the Superuniverses, The Secondary Seconaphim, The Union of Souls
12. Paper 28, Section 5, Number 4: Ministering Spirits of the Superuniverses, The Secondary Seconaphim, The Hearts of Counsel

13. Paper 28, Section 5, Number 5: Ministering Spirits of the Superuniverses, The Secondary Seconaphim, The Joy of Existence
14. Paper 28, Section 5, Number 6: Ministering Spirits of the Superuniverses, The Secondary Seconaphim, The Satisfaction of Service
15. Paper 28, Section 5, Number 7: Ministering Spirits of the Superuniverses, The Secondary Seconaphim, The Discerner of Spirits
16. Paper 28, Section 6, Number 1: Ministering Spirits of the Superuniverses, The Tertiary Seconaphim, The Significance of Origins
17. Paper 28, Section 6, Number 2: Ministering Spirits of the Superuniverses, The Tertiary Seconaphim, The Memory of Mercy
18. Paper 28, Section 6, Number 3: Ministering Spirits of the Superuniverses, The Tertiary Seconaphim, The Import of Time
19. Paper 28, Section 6, Number 4: Ministering Spirits of the Superuniverses, The Tertiary Seconaphim, The Solemnity of Trust
20. Paper 28, Section 6, Number 5: Ministering Spirits of the Superuniverses, The Tertiary Seconaphim, The Sanctity of Service
21. Paper 28, Section 6, Numbers 6 & 7: Ministering Spirits of the Superuniverses, The Tertiary Seconaphim, The Secret of Greatness and the Soul of Goodness

## 4. BRILLIANT EVENING STARS

1. Paper 37, Section 2: Personalities of the Local Universe, The Brilliant Evening Stars

## 5. ARCHANGELS

1. Paper 113, Section 6: Seraphic Guardians of Destiny, Destiny of the Guardian Seraphim
2. Paper 113, Section 6: Seraphic Guardians of Destiny, Guardian Angels After Death

## 7. THE SERAPHIC ORDERS

1. Paper 38, Section 2: Ministering Spirits of the Local Universe, The Seraphim
2. Paper 39, Section 1, Numbers 1 & 2: The Seraphic Hosts, The Supreme Seraphim, Son-Spirit Ministers & Bestowal Attendants
3. Paper 39, Section 1, Number 2: The Seraphic Hosts, The Supreme Seraphim, Court Advisors
4. Paper 39, Section 1, Number 3: The Seraphic Hosts, The Supreme Seraphim, Universe Orientators
5. Paper 39, Section 1, Number 4: The Seraphic Hosts, The Supreme Seraphim, The Teaching Counselors
6. Paper 39, Section 1, Number 5: The Seraphic Hosts, The Supreme Seraphim, Directors of Assignment
7. Paper 39, Section 1, Number 6: The Seraphic Hosts, The Supreme Seraphim, The Recorders
8. Paper 39, Section 1, Number 7: The Seraphic Hosts, The Supreme Seraphim, Unattached Ministers

## 8. THE ANGELIC HOME WORLDS

7. Paper 38, Section 4: Ministering Spirits of the Local Universe, Seraphic Organization
8. Paper 43, Section 0: The Constellations, Introduction
9. Paper 43, Section 0: The Constellations, Introduction
10. Paper 43, Section 1: The Constellations, The Constellation Headquarters
11. Paper 46, Section 2: The Local System Headquarters, Physical Aspects of Jerusem

## 9. THE PLANETARY SERAPHIM

1. Paper 38, Section 1: Ministering Spirits of the Local Universe, Origin of Seraphim
2. Paper 39, Section 5: The Seraphic Hosts, The Planetary Helpers
3. Paper 39, Section 5, Number 1: The Seraphic Hosts, The Planetary Helpers, The Voices of the Garden
4. Paper 39, Section 5, Number 2: The Seraphic Hosts, The Planetary Helpers, The Spirits of Brotherhood
5. Paper 39, Section 5, Number 3: The Seraphic Hosts, The Planetary Helpers, The Souls of Peace
6. Paper 39, Section 5, Number 4: The Seraphic Hosts, The Planetary Helpers, The Spirits of Trust
7. Paper 39, Section 5, Number 5: The Seraphic Hosts, The Planetary Helpers, The Transporters
8. Paper 114, Section 6: Seraphic Planetary Government, The Reserve Corps of Destiny
9. Paper 48, Section 6: The Morontia Life, The Morontia Progressors, Seraphic Evangels
10. Paper 48, Section 6, Number 3: The Morontia Life, The Morontia Progressors, Mind Planners
11. Paper 48, Section 6, Number 4: The Morontia Life, The Morontia Progressors, Morontia Counselors
12. Paper 48, Section 6, Number 5: The Morontia Life, Morontia World Seraphim—Transition Ministers, Technicians
13. Paper 48, Section 6, Number 6: The Morontia Life, The Morontia Progressors, Recorder-Teachers
14. Paper 48, Section 6, Number 7: The Morontia Life, The Morontia Progressors, Ministering Reserves

## 10. GUARDIAN ANGELS

1. Paper 113, Section 3: Relation to Other Spirit Influences

## 11. CHERUBIM AND SANOBIM

1. Paper 38, Section 7: Ministering Spirits of the Local Universe, Cherubim and Sanobim
2. Paper 38, Section 7: Ministering Spirits of the Local Universe, Cherubim and Sanobim

3. Paper 38, Section 7: Ministering Spirits of the Local Universe, Cherubim and Sanobim
4. Paper 38, Section 7: Ministering Spirits of the Local Universe, Cherubim and Sanobim
5. Paper 38, Section 7: Ministering Spirits of the Local Universe, Cherubim and Sanobim

## 12. MIDWAYERS

1. Paper 38, Section 9: Ministering Spirits of the Local Universe, The Midway Creatures
2. Paper 38, Section 9: Ministering Spirits of the Local Universe, The Midway Creatures
3. Paper 38, Section 9: Ministering Spirits of the Local Universe, The Midway Creatures
4. Paper 38, Section 9: Ministering Spirits of the Local Universe, The Midway Creatures
5. Paper 38, Section 9: Ministering Spirits of the Local Universe, The Midway Creatures
6. Paper 38, Section 9: Ministering Spirits of the Local Universe, The Midway Creatures
7. Paper 38, Section 9: Ministering Spirits of the Local Universe, The Midway Creatures
8. Paper 38, Section 9: Ministering Spirits of the Local Universe, The Midway Creatures

## 13. ORGANIZATION AND VELOCITY

1. Paper 39, Section 2: The Seraphic Hosts, Superior Seraphim
2. Paper 39, Section 3: The Seraphic Hosts, The Transporters
3. Paper 23, Section 3: The Solitary Messengers, Time and Space Services of Solitary Messengers

# ABOUT THE AUTHOR

Michael Vincent spent years searching for answers that religion couldn't provide. Then he discovered *The Urantia Book*—a dense revelation that answered his questions with a coherence he'd never encountered.

His work translates this complex material into books anyone can absorb. Not spiritual platitudes—specific, detailed information about how reality actually works.

*The Angelic Orders* is part of that project. Other books cover death, Jesus, human origins, and the structure of the universe itself.

michaelvincentauthor.com

instagram.com/michaelvincent_author

tiktok.com/@michael.vincent.author

youtube.com/@MichaelVincent-Author

amazon.com/author/havona-press

## ALSO BY MICHAEL VINCENT

*The Missing Years: The Real Story of Jesus Beyond the Gospels* (The *Universe Maker from Nazareth* series, Book One)

*Where We Go When We Die: Life After Death Across the Universe*

*Fusion with God: The Path to Immortality*

Upcoming Books:

*The Public Ministry: The Real Story of Jesus Beyond the Gospels* (The *Universe Maker from Nazareth* series, Book Two)

*The Final Week: The Real Story of Jesus Beyond the Gospels* (The *Universe Maker from Nazareth* series, Book Three)

*The Nine Races: The Forgotten Origin of Humanity*

*Before Humans: The Drama of World-Making*

*Marcus Aurelius, Rodan of Alexandria, and Jesus of Nazareth: A Philosopher's Journey*